S0-ATP-616

The
INFINITE WAY LETTERS
1956

By
Joel S. Goldsmith

DeVorss & Company, Publisher

Copyright © 1992
by Thelma G. McDonald

All rights reserved. No part of this book may be reproduced in any form
without permission in writing from the publisher, except by a reviewer
who may quote brief passages for review purposes.

British edition published in 1956
DeVorss & Company reprint, 1992

ISBN: 0-87516-643-1

DeVorss & Company, Publisher
P.O. Box 550
Marina del Rey, CA 90294

Printed in the United States of America

INFINITE WAY LETTERS

Except the Lord build the house, they
labor in vain that build it.

Psalm 127

Illumination dissolves all material ties and binds
men together with the golden chains of spiritual
understanding; it acknowledges only the leadership
of the Christ; it has no ritual or rule but the divine,
impersonal universal Love; no other worship than
the inner flame that is ever lit at the shrine of Spirit.
This union is the free state of spiritual brotherhood.
The only restraint is the discipline of Soul, therefore
we know liberty without license; we are a united
universe without physical limits; a divine service to
God without ceremony or creed. The illumined walk
without fear—by Grace.

(From the book *The Infinite Way*.
Published by George Allen & Unwin
Ltd.)

CONTENTS

CHAP.   PAGE

1. WITHINNESS   9
   The Ninth Commandment—Treatment—
   Note to Practitioners and Advanced Stu-
   dents—The Spiritual Path.

2. GOD IS THE SOUL OF MAN . . .   28
   Spiritual Preparation—Spiritual Guidance
   —Holiday in Africa.

3. THE PART WE PLAY   49
   Seek Within—Meditation—Seeking Within
   Reveals the Nature of Prayer—Teaching
   The Infinite Way to Children—Across
   the Desk—Oneness.

4. NEITHER GOOD NOR EVIL . . .   76
   The Middle Path—Judge Not According
   to the Appearance, but Judge Righteous
   Judgment—Oneness with God—The In-
   finite Way Lesson for Children: Love—
   Aloha—Across the Desk—The Principle in
   Healing.

5. A BEHOLDER   102
   The Infinite Way Lesson for Children:
   Peace—Across the Desk.

6. IN GOD'S PRESENCE IS FULLNESS OF LIFE   126
   Faith—The Infinite Way Lesson for
   Children: Obedience—Anandashram: a
   Spiritual Haven—Across the Desk—The
   New Infinite Way.

7. TRANSITION FROM LAW TO GRACE .   150
   Receptivity—The Infinite Way Lesson for
   Children: The Universality of Truth—The
   True Basis of Religion.

8. CONTEMPLATIVE MEDITATION . . 175
        The Middle Path—Be Taught of God—
        What is Religion?

9. SPIRITUAL ILLUMINATION—THE WAY OF
        HARMONY 203
        Enlightened Prayer — Practicing the
        Presence.

10. THE DEMONSTRATION OF GOD . . 218
        The Fifteenth Chapter of John—Spiritual
        Power.

11. SCRIPTURAL PRINCIPLES . . . 231
        The 147th Psalm—The 46th Psalm—Love
        —A Prayer—Spiritual Attainment—Across
        the Desk.

12. THE CHRIST 252
        The Monastic Life—The Bridge Over
        Which We Travel.

CHAPTER ONE

WITHINNESS

AT this stage of our unfoldment the time has come when we must relinquish our old theological beliefs and come to understand the nature of God. This I give to you: God is! God is good! God is omnipresent! The allness of the presence of God, in Its infinite goodness, power, intelligence, wisdom, and love, is present—here, where you are and where I am. "Closer is He than breathing, and nearer than hands and feet." None of us can make it so, and none of us can prevent its being so—it is so! *God is!*

Is it not foolish to believe that God will do something for you that He might not do for your neighbor; or that God will do something tomorrow that He is not already doing today? There is no reason to believe that God is withholding your good, and therefore it is useless to go to God as if you were seeking to influence Him to do something that He is not already doing. In order to avail yourselves of the abundant flow of good, and bring it into your experience, it is necessary to open your own consciousness to the receptivity of the presence, power, and activity of God.

We must not seek to obtain God's goodness. Instead, we must agree that God's goodness is embodied within us, that the goodness and allness of God constitute our very being. This is beautifully stated in the words of the beloved poet, Browning:

> Truth is within ourselves; it takes no rise
> From outward things, whate're you may believe.
> There is an inmost center in us all,
> Where truth abides in fulness; . . . and, to KNOW,
> Rather consists in opening out a way
> Whence the imprisoned splendour may escape,
> Than in effecting entry for a light
> Supposed to be without.
>
> *Paracelsus:* ROBERT BROWNING[1]

Many people believe that they are seeking companionship, and because they are lonely they often ask for help, but that really is not what they mean at all. They are seeking companions. If it were companionship they desired they would not have to ask for help, because *companionship is not something outside their own being*! Companionship is within you and, instead of looking to someone else to express it, *you must express it*! Start with the understanding that companionship is a quality of God which is embodied within you and begin to express it, right where you are. As you open out a way for companionship to flow you will find many opportunities will be given; and the companionship that *flows out from you* is the same that comes back to you.

In like manner, where will you find integrity,

[1] From *The Collected Works of Robert Browning.*

loyalty, and fidelity if you do not already possess these qualities within your own being? Never permit yourself to look to another to express these qualities. Each man's life is his own, and whether or not he wishes to express these innate characteristics of his higher nature is his own affair, but since no one can hurt you by any lack of integrity or loyalty the injury is to the one not expressing them. Even if someone were to deprive you temporarily of something that is rightfully yours, be assured that you will not be hurt by the loss, and your good will continue to unfold.

Just as you do not look to anyone for companionship, integrity, loyalty, or fidelity, do not look to anyone for gratitude. Expect it of no one, but rather look for gratitude within yourself—express it, and watch it return. "Cast thy bread upon the waters; for thou shalt find it after many days." It is a spiritual law that the good that comes into your experience is the reflex action of the good that flows from you. The love, companionship, friendship, cooperation, and understanding that you express from within is the substance of the bread of life that you cast upon the waters, and it comes back to you abundantly.

In a degree, each of us is withholding these qualities with which God has imbued us. If you will watch a little child you will find it spontaneously expressing love, trust, faith, joy, playfulness—the very things we would love to have in our own hearts. But human experience has built a shell around us, and we keep these inherent God-qualities all bottled up inside. Because someone has injured us, we hold back for fear that all the rest of the world will do the same, and as the years pass each of us withdraws more and more, withholding a little love and friendship here, a little faith and trust there, until we become nothing but a prison-house for these splendors of God, and we are afraid to let them out. Why that reserve, that holding back? We are children of God, all equal in the sight of the Father. White or black, Jew or Gentile, we are all one in Christ Jesus. God has constituted His qualities as our own being, and when we understand that, we do not have to go to God for anything necessary for our unfoldment and fulfilment. Our work in life is opening consciousness to the inflow and outflow of this spiritual Presence and Power. We must re-establish that joyful trust and love with which we were endowed as babes—that trust and love which holds out its little hands, even to a stranger—so that we can express it to the world, letting that which comes back be the abundant return of that which we have cast upon the waters.

Your good does not *come* to you—your good is the reflex action of the spiritual Presence. By way of illustration: suppose, in some miraculous manner, I could bring God Himself right here beside me as I speak to you. Would you not immediately say: "Lucky fellow! Your problems are over. You have God, and with God all things are possible. You have that which multiplies the loaves and fishes; that which is the healer, the resurrection. You have life eternal. You have God, what more can you have?" And you would be absolutely right! If I can become quiet and still within until I feel the divine spiritual impulse as an *actual reality*, a Presence and Power within me, then I am indeed a lucky fellow. From that time on nothing of a negative nature can happen to me, because the presence of God is annihilation to even a suspicion of a belief of a selfhood apart from God. This is the secret of the entire message of The Infinite Way, but each student must achieve for himself this realization of the actual presence of God, and henceforth let good unfold from within his own being.

We have no need to demonstrate supply, companionship, home, employment, or anything else on the face of the globe. We have but one demonstration to make, and that is the conscious awareness or "feeling" of oneness or union with God. This is not an easy matter, but it can be accomplished by each one of you, even if, in the beginning, it may seem to be only a tiny degree of awareness. However, as you continue in the practice, the degree of God consciousness increases and becomes greater, more assured and sustained, until undoubtedly the day will come when you can be like unto the Master who always maintained conscious union with the Father within. If you will remember, the Master did not have to turn the stones into bread: He just waited, and let the Father perform whatever miracles were necessary.

Many, many times in the writings and recordings of the message of The Infinite Way, you will read and hear these scriptural truths: "Thou wilt keep him in perfect peace, whose mind is stayed on thee"; "Trust in the Lord with all thine heart; and lean not unto thine own understanding. In all thy ways acknowledge him, and he shall direct thy paths"; "Abide in me, and I in you. As the branch cannot bear fruit of itself, except it abide in the vine; no more can ye, except ye abide in me." If you abide in the Word of God, and let this Word abide in you, you will be as a branch that is one with the Vine, that is one with the Godhead, and you will bear much fruit. As you continue *to dwell* "in the secret place of the most High," you will find that it is not a matter of God's doing something for you—it is a matter of maintaining conscious oneness with God, keeping your mind stayed on God, acknowledging God in all your ways, abiding in the Word and letting the Word abide in you.

In actual practice, this means awakening each morning and veritably bringing the presence of God right into the room with you in the realization that "This is the day the Lord hath made." Instead of bringing to consciousness your problems, sins, and inharmonies, bring God into your awareness in the realization that God is with you throughout the day. You can face any problem or task in the realization that you do not face it alone, "For he performeth the thing that is appointed for me." God is your supply, forgiveness, life, love. Emmanuel—God with us—is that which enables you to be, to do, to prosper. Consciously realize that God's presence goes before you, and when going about your affairs consciously know that the Christ is greeting you through every individual encountered. *Acknowledge Him in all thy ways* and you will be obeying Paul's injunction to "pray without ceasing." In God you will have a friend, a big brother, the Father within; and you will come into the realization, as did Paul, "I can do all things through Christ which strengtheneth me."

As you persist in the practice of the Presence you are carried along by its beauty and harmony, and a day will dawn when "you" no longer exist. Then there will be no need to think about God—there will be only God, functioning as your individual being, thinking, being, knowing, living through you, and then it is literally true: ". . . I live; yet not I, but Christ liveth in me: and the life which I now live in the flesh I live by the faith of the Son of God. . . ."

As you behold these unfolding glories you may be inclined to wonder what you have done to deserve such blessings. You have done nothing. God's grace never is bestowed upon the human being, but upon the spiritual being which is revealed when the limited, finite, human self has been dissolved. When we let God through in order that He may function as our being, we are no longer human beings. When we no longer hold the splendors of love and trust and faith imprisoned in reserve; when we cease to condemn and find fault with the people of the world, but meet them in a spontaneous feeling of love and joy; when we have learned to forgive the offenses that are aimed at us personally, religiously, racially, nationally; when we acknowledge that the world is returning exactly what we send out to it—then it is that we are children of God.

But ye are not in the flesh, but in the Spirit, if so be that the Spirit of God dwell in you. . . .

For as many as are led by the Spirit of God, they are the sons of God.

Romans 8:9, 14

The Ninth Commandment

Ordinarily the Commandment, "Thou shalt not bear false witness against thy neighbor," is understood to mean that one should not bear tales or repeat scandal and gossip about one's neighbor, but the spiritual meaning is much more profound than that. To bear false witness against your neighbor is to accept him as a human being. Even to say that your neighbor is good and healthy is to bear false witness against him because, by so doing, you are holding him as a limited, finite human being who was born and will die, who may be good today and bad tomorrow. Obedience to the Ninth Commandment is to understand that your neighbor is immortal and eternal, possessing only the qualities of God, which are spiritual.

In God there are no opposites. That which is God is infinite and eternal: therefore, it cannot be white or black, good or bad, sick or well, beautiful or ugly. That which is God is an invisible spiritual being—and that is what you are and what I am. The *I that I am* is invisible; *I am* in and of God; *I am* spiritual; *I am* perfect. God constitutes my individual identity, and even though I may sometimes forget and permit my actions to belie that truth, nevertheless that does not change the fact that in essence and identity and being that is what *I am*. Anything short of that can be blamed on the humanhood which has built up a shell that prevents the real

16

spiritual identity being made manifest. I, Joel, am invisible. That which you see is the body, and if you look only at that, you are judging unrighteous judgment. However, if you become still and quiet until you arrive at a state of spiritual realization, you see me as *I am*—spiritual, complete, and perfect.

When a practitioner on the spiritual path works for you, he does not work for health, nor against disease; he does not work for supply, nor against lack; he does not work for goodness, nor against sinfulness. Rather, he closes his eyes to your humanhood, turns completely from it, and tabernacles with God until he attains a state of realization in which is beheld your spiritual nature, your spiritual being, your spiritual Selfhood. This is what takes place in healing.

The lessons on treatment, as presented in the various writings, are very necessary until such time as you achieve a solid foundation in the letter of truth, and a thorough understanding of what you are leading up to. There is one thing of which you must be sure: you are not leading up to a blind faith! At the beginning of your study and practice, you may find at least fifteen minutes are necessary for a treatment, but gradually the time will be shortened until, after awhile, the average treatment will not require more than two minutes, and, later, but a few seconds. The reason for this is simple: when you first begin to master the multiplication tables it takes time to figure out 12×12, but after you have studied a while the immediate answer is 144.

Just as it takes considerable time to learn the

multiplication tables, so also it takes time to learn the nature of spiritual being—what God is, what the individual is, and what the relationship is, what the law of God is, and how it operates. That is why you include these in your treatments, and although it may take a few minutes longer, never hesitate to spend all the time that is necessary until you arrive at that moment of release. After the letter of truth has been consciously brought to mind, you will arrive at a place where none of that enters your thought. You will become very still and quiet and silent within, and if you think anything at all it will be the word "God"—God is life eternal; God is the only law; God is the only being. God—God—nothing but God, and in that stillness there will steal over you that divine impulse which is an intuition, an assurance, a knowing, and in that sense of release you will have attained an awareness of spiritual reality, which is your true being and mine.

You are a pure, infinite, immortal, and eternal spiritual being—invisible to this world. You will never die, but will always exist as an individual state of consciousness, ever progressing in spiritual development and unfoldment. There is no mysterious God to do this for you, so whatever takes place to benefit you is the result of your own improved state of consciousness. But once you learn this truth the out-picturing will become progressively better than it is at this moment. This higher state of consciousness is attained by constant practice. In all your relationships at home, in business, driving or shopping, *it is imperative that you consciously behold the invisible spiritual identity of every person you meet.* In this practice you do not see the body; you do not see male or female, rich or poor, sick or well. Instead, you see a light—a light which shines forth from each person's eyes, and you become consciously aware of the very Child of God behind those "windows of the Soul."

Much can be accomplished through association with your teacher or practitioner and with others on the path, and you will benefit greatly from their state of consciousness. Much progress can be made by living in the Writings and the Recordings, but you must be careful not to lean too much. The disciples benefited from association with the Master, but not enough, and most of them committed grave blunders. It was only after the Master went away that they awakened to the realization that each must find his own union with God. This is no work for a lazy man! *You must develop your own state of consciousness!* You must learn that God constitutes your being, and you must behold that same spiritual being behind the eyes of every individual in this world, even though they themselves may not recognize it.

When the Master said, "Arise, and take thy bed, and go thy way into thine house," he did not see a man bound by a diseased body—he saw only the unfettered Soul, and was saying, in effect: "You, the Soul—arise! Take up thy body, and walk!" It is inevitable that as you continue in this work you will be called into sick rooms and into hospitals and prisons, and always you must remember not to judge by appearances. When you have learned to see the Soul of the Child of God shining through those pain-filled eyes, you too can say: "Pick up that body, and walk out of this prison-house of beliefs!" This can happen, however, only as you and I, individually, "pray without ceasing"—but that does not mean praying *to* God *for* something. Prayer is a recognition of God as the life of every individual. Prayer is the awareness of ever-present good. Prayer is an acknowledgment of God in all thy ways. Prayer is understanding God as the only power operating in consciousness. It is in the understanding and application of these spiritual principles that you live in obedience to the Ninth Commandment and, thereby, bear *true* witness unto thy neighbor.

TREATMENT

Part One

The nature of all inharmony exists only as suggestion or appearance—an illusory sense. To treat spiritually is to reinterpret experience as it comes into range of your awareness. Consciously to know the truth about God and Its creation is the healing treatment which determines the harmony of your existence. It is imperative that you learn to reinterpret every situation or seemingly discordant condition in the understanding that God is the substance, law, and action of all true being and, therefore, you will not fear appearances of any nature. The activity of this truth in your consciousness constitutes the law unto every situation or condition.

When faced with any suggestion of a selfhood or condition apart from God, turn to God in thought, ponder these truths, and meditate upon them—always remembering, however, that memorizing or reciting these words is not treatment! Let Truth reveal Itself from within your own being, in ever new and fresh thoughts, ideas, unfoldments, and revelations. The scriptural truth, ". . . greater is he that is in you, than he that is in the world," is the assurance that your very consciousness of Truth is the treatment to every appearance of evil.

Perhaps some member of your family is ill, or experiencing some sense of discord. Immediately your thought goes to God, and you are reminded that the harmonious and eternal, creative principle of Life appears as the life of every individual. Therefore, that which claims existence as disease or discord can have no substance, no power, no cause—hence, no reality. As you understand God as the one infinite Being, the creative Principle and Substance of all that *is*, you do not accept any appearance of discord as actually being a part of life or body. Whenever you behold any appearance of error whatsoever, your reaction will be the same.

An understanding treatment never concerns itself with getting rid of or destroying discord, but includes only the realization of God and Its harmonies, perfection, substance, and law, and, as a consequence, the unreal or illusory nature of any appearance or suggestion of evil. If you will go back into the Old Testament, you will read of the siege of Jerusalem, where Hezekiah, the king of Judah, tells his people: "Be strong and courageous, be not afraid nor dismayed for the king of Assyria, nor for all the multitude that is with him: for there be more with us than with him: With him is an arm of flesh; but with us is the Lord our God to help us and to fight our battles." The understanding treatment does not battle error or seek to destroy it, but knows that the infinite and eternal nature of individual being makes impossible any condition or action that does not have its source in the Spirit.

Your treatments will be fruitful in proportion to your faith in the Infinite Invisible. This faith grows and waxes strong as you realize that the infinite nature of eternal life makes God, the one Mind or divine Consciousness, the actual substance of all good. Heretofore, it has been believed that God sends or gives your good, but now you know that *God appears as your good*! God does not *send* security or peace—*God is security and peace;* God does not *give* employment—*God is the very acitivity of your work;* God does not *send* supply—*God is the substance of all forms of supply;* God does not *give* family and companions—*God appears as family and friends!*

There is within you that which sees what eyes can never witness, hears what ears can never hear, and it is this intuitive inner Soul faculty which enables you to see through appearances, pierce the veil of illusion, dispel the sense of discord, discern the harmony of God and the spiritual perfection of all being. Spiritual treatment is based upon this inner Soul faculty, and when made a regular and frequent part of your daily life it develops an inner awareness and constant assurance of a divine Presence accompanying you at every step. It provides you with infinite wisdom and divine protection from the discords of sense. It reveals harmony and peace as ever present and, eventually, an insight into the kingdom of God on earth. Treatment, rightly understood, develops the inner faculties so that your spiritual resources become the substance and activity of your outer experience and enables you to draw upon this eternal, infinite, invisible Source for whatever healing, supply, or protection is necessary, rather than depending on outer forms for your good.

The object of the message of The Infinite Way is the development and revelation of these inner spiritual resources of the individual; that you may ever prove that "I have meat to eat that ye know not of"; *that your good is the continuous unfolding of your own consciousness*, always appearing in the form necessary to the experience of the moment.

Son, thou art ever with me, and all that I [the inner Self] have is thine.

Part Two

None of the things so feared and dreaded by the world can cause inharmony in your experience unless you endow them with the power to do so, but you give them that power whenever you believe that because you have been a bit resentful or envious or unkind you must expect some dire result. Countless people are holding themselves under so-called "laws" of sin and disease by saying, "My envy, my jealousy, my hatred is causing this discord." Even practitioners sometimes bind their patients in the belief

23

of disease and discord by giving power to mental-cause. Mental-cause is no more power than is physical cause, but if you make such laws for yourself you will surely bring them into being. If you believe that germs have power to cause disease so it will be in your experience. On the other hand, if you believe that germs do not have power, but that wrong thinking does, you have made that a law unto yourself. If the germ theory is a belief then, likewise, the mental-cause theory is a belief, in spite of the fact that, to human sense, worry produces ulcers and germs cause disease. But—does that make them laws, or does it make them beliefs which are accepted as laws?

In the world where germs and mental causes are accepted as law, disease and inharmony are rampant. Regardless of what laws the world may set up for itself, *there is only one law*, and it is this: God is! God is Life; God is Love; God is Power; God is Spirit. God is infinite spiritual Law: therefore, neither error nor sin nor disease nor death has power to perpetuate itself because there is no law to sustain them!

As you rise into the spiritual realm you will more clearly understand the words of Genesis: "And God saw every thing that he had made, and, behold, it was very good." Since God made all that was made, and all that God made is good, that which God did not make was never made. There is no evil presence, no evil power, no evil cause. When you know the truth that disease or error has no cause, no continuity, no being, no law, it will have no effect.

24

You may be assured that God is functioning perfectly even while hospitals are overflowing with the sick; while wars wipe out millions; while infection and contagion encircle the globe; while innocent children are born deaf and blind. Why is this so? Of what good is God to all these people who seem as branches that are cut off and withereth? The answer is given by the Psalmist who says that you must *dwell* in the secret place of the most High; by the Master who says that you must *abide* in this Truth, and let this Truth abide in you; by Paul who says that you must *pray without ceasing*! It is absolutely necessary that you know, consciously, that *God is the only power*—and this is the truth that will make you free!

A Note to Practitioners and Advanced Students

When a claim of error arises, the metaphysician or truth student is quick to answer with a denial, or with some sort of affirmation of truth. In the earlier stages of one's study and practice this is well, and it is necessary, but the practitioner or advanced student should not meet any case in this way.

Since every claim is an argument, to answer back, either with a denial or an affirmation, is to use argument against the argument, and in this way a battle is enjoined. From the standpoint of the higher understanding of spiritual practice, one should not make any denial, nor should one voice a truth in contradiction of an error. To voice a truth in contradiction of an error is meeting the

25

error head-on, and it is using the very weapon of the error. The error is an argument, and the moment one answers back, even with a word of truth, the battle has begun.

Under no circumstances should an advanced student make a declaration of truth to refute an argument of error. Resist the temptation to know any truth, and when presented with an argument of a negative nature stand fast without permitting a single thought of affirmation or denial to enter your mind. By thus standing without mentally refuting the appearance, you attain an attitude of receptivity and Truth quickly fills your consciousness.

This is the "Middle Path" referred to in the Writings and taught in the Practitioners' Classes.

The Spiritual Path

Those of you who are serious students of The Infinite Way will be most anxious to share this truth with your loved ones, and you will yearn to take them also into this heaven. But this is not always possible. Even if it were possible to present this message to thousands of people at one time, only a few would be capable of receiving it. But to those who can receive it, this message is life itself because the Spirit within has drawn them unto their own.

By your example you will be able to influence some of your loved ones, with marked improvement evident in their lives, but others will desert you, because you will be living in a realm of consciousness far removed from their present state. No longer will you be able to converse with them about germs and mental-causes, the latest movies and newspaper scandals, because these things will seem superficial. Instead, you will want to be with those of your own true household, with whom you can share these truths, and where the conversation is kept in heaven. This happens to every one who earnestly devotes himself to the spiritual path, and although it may be a lonely and heartbreaking experience for a time, the ultimate unfoldment of truth compensates to a far greater degree than anything of the materialistic world that you may lose.

CHAPTER TWO

GOD IS THE SOUL OF MAN

How excellent is thy lovingkindness, O God! therefore the children of men put their trust under the shadow of thy wings. They shall be abundantly satisfied with the fatness of thy house; and thou shalt make them drink of the river of thy pleasures. For with thee is the fountain of life: in thy light shall we see light. O continue thy lovingkindness unto them that know thee; and thy righteousness to the upright in heart. Let not the foot of pride come against me, and let not the hand of the wicked remove me. There are the workers of iniquity fallen: they are cast down, and shall not be able to rise.

Psalms 36:7-12

Fret not thyself because of evildoers, neither be thou envious against the workers of iniquity. For they shall soon be cut down like the grass, and wither as the green herb. Trust in the Lord, and do good; so shalt thou dwell in the land, and verily thou shalt be fed. Delight thyself also in the Lord; and he shall give thee the desires of thine heart. Commit thy way unto the Lord; trust also in him; and he shall bring it to pass. And he shall bring forth thy righteousness as the light, and thy judgment as the noonday. Rest in the Lord, and wait patiently for him: fret not thyself because of him who prospereth in his way, because of the man who bringeth wicked devices to pass. Cease from anger, and forsake wrath: fret not thyself in any wise to do evil. For evildoers shall be cut off: but those that wait upon the Lord, they shall inherit the earth.

Psalms 37:1-9

Part One

IN order to know God, to understand God, to place your faith fully in Him, it must be understood that God is the Soul of man, and that *God is the Soul of you!* The grace of God is universal—"for he maketh his sun to rise on the evil and on the good, and sendeth rain on the just and on the unjust." Everyone, saint or sinner, has a Soul; and this Soul is pure, never depleted, never lacks, never has been touched or tainted by human thoughts, deeds, or conditions. In this understanding, you are not putting your trust in something unknown, afar off, or difficult to obtain. It is because you do not realize that God is your Soul, that seeking and reaching out for God sometimes separates you from your good, because you are thinking of God as something separate and apart from your own being.

Fear is based on the belief of a God afar off, of a God who may not be aware of your needs; and it is only when you really know God as your own Soul that you confidently trust everything to Him. In the realization that God is your Soul, that which is responsible for your being on earth, and which is responsible for your continuing unto eternity, can you fear, can you doubt, can you place confidence elsewhere? Once you recognize God to be your Soul, never again will it be necessary to reach out to God, or fear that God is not with you, for then you know, "Closer is He than breathing, and nearer than hands and feet." Once you realize that God is your Soul, you can rest, knowing that where I am—here, in the withinness of your own being—is your own Soul, and *that Soul is God!*

When some experience of the world tempts you with its claim of lack of health, lack of supply or safety, lack of peace, there is just one place to turn for the resurrection of your good, and that is to the Soul. Whenever tempted with illness of any nature, realize that there is no health in the body—health is in the Soul: the body is but the receiving place for that health; that place where the health of the Soul is made manifest. Whenever tempted by lack or limitation, realize that supply is not money in the bank—supply is in your Soul, that storehouse of all good, which also is that center through which God pours Its good to all others. As long as you know that your own Soul is the storehouse of infinite good, never will you be separated from any part of God's grace.

Miracles occur once you realize that safety, security, supply, and health are not dependent upon shelters, investments, or body; but that safety, security, supply, and health are within your very own Soul. All good is in your Soul, and is reflected in the mind and body.

You can turn from God only in belief, never in truth, because you cannot walk away from your own Soul. If you make your bed in heaven or in hell, your Soul is there; if you walk in the shadow of death, your Soul is with you—It can never leave you nor forsake you. God is the Soul of man—of sinner as well as saint. Even the greatest sinner finds his good the moment he realizes it is not to be found in the outer world, but within himself. Then it is that the Soul speaks: "I was with you when you were feasting on the husks; when you were turned from Me, and thought you had left Me. I am with you alway, even unto the end of the world."

For long years we have acknowledged that all good is in God, but sometimes we forget, momentarily, and in confusion and indecision wonder how to reach God, which way to turn. The Soul of man— your Soul and mine—is infinite wisdom, infinite intelligence, divine love, and never have we become separated from It. ". . . the place where thou standest is holy ground,"—God is where you are; the Soul, the storehouse of all good is within us. Never, even for a moment, believe that there is any way for God to be separated from you, unaware of the immediate needs of every second. Once the idea dawns in consciousness that God is your Soul, you no longer look elsewhere for your good, but by turning to that infinite storehouse, the Soul, and drawing upon It, you will be rightfully guided and supplied with all that is required for every experience.

Part Two

God, the Soul of man, speaks to the listening ear as Soul unto Soul, as Heart unto Heart:

Never more shalt thou fear. Nevermore must thou doubt. Nevermore turn to man whose breath is in his nostrils. Nevermore turn to the outside world—*for I am with you*! I have been with you since the world began, to form you in the image and likeness of God; to send you forever about the Father's business. Look unto *Me*, the Soul of thy being, and be saved! Look unto *Me* for wisdom and guidance, for safety and security and support, for healing and for comfort. Look unto *Me* for resurrection and, finally, for ascension.

Never doubt that the Voice will speak when you are listening. Never doubt that the finger of Grace on the hand of Love will touch you when need be. The Voice will utter Itself unto you; the hand of the Father will be the power; the love of God will be the means. Always remember that your good is in *Me*, the Soul, and in all thy ways turn unto *Me*. God's grace flows to all men everywhere, wherever the listening ear is developed, wherever there is one to recognize that he cannot falter or stumble because of this divine Presence within his own being.

The Soul speaks unto Soul, saying: "All this is true of you and of me. We are held by an invisible bond of Love. We are one. Awake thou that sleepest, and find *Me*, the Soul within you." As the Soul thus speaks, we are awakened to the realization of God's most precious gift to man.

The Soul of your being is the source, the activity, the substance, the immortal life; and nothing shall enter which defileth or maketh a lie; there is no place where even a suggestion of evil can find an abiding place. "... yet in my flesh shall I see God," and as you turn to the Soul for the unfolding of your good, It appears as the health of your flesh; intelligence of your intelligence; life of your life. All this flows from the Soul, and is made manifest in the flesh.

"Look unto me, and be ye saved, all the ends of the earth: for I am God, and there is none else." Look only unto *Me*, not unto the men nor the thoughts and things of the world. No more must you voice the doubts and fears of the world, but speak the Word of God, the Word of Truth. No more must you hear the doubts and fears of the world, but listen for the still, small Voice. Hold the Word of God high in the mind and in the heart. Let the name of God be upon your lips—let it always be *God—God—God*, in the knowledge that all good is in Him. In all thy ways acknowledge Him, whom to know aright is life eternal. "And call no man your Father upon the earth: for one is your Father, which is in heaven." God, the Soul, the Father within, is the creative energy of all being, and therefore of your individual mind and body; the creative urge and activity of your world experience. Thus it is understood that as you sow to the flesh—to the external realm, the form—you will reap corruption; but as you sow to the Spirit—the Soul within—you will reap life everlasting.

It may be difficult, at first, to believe and understand that there is an invisible Presence and Power maintaining, guiding, and governing you harmoniously; being your shelter and fortress; your bread, wine, meat, water—and it may take a while to become accustomed to this old, yet new idea; but when the invisible Presence, the Soul, is realized to be the fount of life, you have, indeed, entered the kingdom of heaven. The price of demonstration is that this first be maintained in consciousness, sacredly and secretly; that is, you must secretly and silently declare these truths about yourself, and then about all individuals with whom you come in contact, be they human, animal, vegetable, or mineral. Know the truth that *God is the Soul of man*, and voice it for the benefit of every individual, far and near, who comes within range of your consciousness. Use it, realize it, with every experience of a personal, national, or international nature; but keep it secret, silent, sacred, knowing the truth that God, the Soul, is ever revealing Its will to man.

Never voice this truth in words, however, except to those of thine own "household." Otherwise, you are casting your pearls before the unprepared thought, and they are liable to be trampled under foot. No one can value the truth, no one can accept it nor even believe it, until he is ready for it. The human mind rejects spiritual truth because the things of God are foolishness to man's intellect, and it is only when he has opened his Soul to truth that he is able to receive it. Do not give this truth to the unprepared thought, but voice it silently, blessing everyone, friend, enemy, and believer alike, by secretly and silently knowing that this is the truth of their innermost being. Then it is that the Soul speaks unto the Soul.

Where two or more are "gathered together in my name," we are come for the purpose of opening our souls to God—opening consciousness that we may be filled. Therefore, any word of truth that is voiced is received, accepted, and responded to. If we were to give this to passers-by they would reject it because they do not look in this direction; they have many other sources of authority in which they believe, and that is their individual demonstration. You bless them only if you address them in the secret place of the most High—there the Soul can speak to Soul and not be rejected.

In the silence, speak to the Soul of your children, and even of your pets, and notice how they respond to the Word of Truth, without a single uttered word. As you continue in this practice, always recognizing the spiritual nature of the one you are addressing, you will be able to speak to the Soul of adults, and they also will respond, and although they may not acknowledge it, being unaware of what has happened, their response will be by way of greater health, purity, or supply. In the silence, gently let the Soul speak unto Soul: "Thou art fair; thou art pure. In thee is no evil; in thee the world beliefs have no place. Thou art the beloved Son of God, made in His image and likeness, sent to earth to be about the Father's business. *Thou art He.*" Oh! the power of these words, whispered unto the Soul of man when his intellectual mind is not listening!

Nothing is more wonderful than the realization of this truth. It purifies one from head to foot, and pervades every detail of one's experience. But that is as nothing compared to what happens when one Soul speaks to the Soul of another, recognizing only the purity, the infinity, the perfection of individual being, in the realization that *God is the Soul of man!*

Spiritual Preparation

And he spake many things unto them in parables, saying, Behold, a sower went forth to sow; and when he sowed, some seeds fell by the way side, and the fowls came and devoured them up: Some fell upon stony places, where they had not much earth: and forthwith they sprung up, because they had no deepness of earth: And when the sun was up, they were scorched; and because they had no root, they withered away. And some fell among thorns; and the thorns sprung up, and choked them: But other fell into good ground, and brought forth fruit, some an hundredfold, some sixtyfold, some thirtyfold. Who hath ears to hear, let him hear.

Matthew 13:3-9

When the message of The Infinite Way was given me, as the result of many years of healing work, meditation, and inner spiritual unfoldment, it was also revealed that this message could not be entirely intellectually imparted; that the import of The Infinite Way could not be grasped by the mind alone, but that there must be a natural or developed spiritual consciousness before a true response could come forth. Many times did I try to impart the message to *students close to me before the soil had been sufficiently prepared, but in every case I witnessed that the seed withered and died, and there was no spiritual fruitage.

Then, as the call came to lecture and teach, it was

given me to prepare the soil for the truth of The Infinite Way. Just as I spent sixteen years in the healing work before *The Infinite Way* was written, so that no word of it need be changed—so have I now spent ten years in preparing consciousness for the Word which springs into flesh—the Truth which appears visibly as harmony, joy, peace, and life eternal. By means of the Writings, the Tape Recordings, and the Closed Class work, consciousness has been prepared for receptivity to the Word. Five years ago, when what we call "the Middle Path" was given to our students in class work, the way was prepared for the next step—realization.

To those who may now or hereafter become students of The Infinite Way, these writings and recordings will provide the necessary enrichment of consciousness—the necessary preparation of consciousness—so that the Word embodied in the message may be grasped, realized, and lived. To The Infinite Way students of today, the time has come to leave your nets—to give up even the most cherished beliefs of the past, and consciously *enter The Infinite Way*. With the help of those students who already have received this light, I will devote these coming years to your full awakening. Many of you are prepared, by virtue of the devotion given to study, meditation, and practice, to fully understand and demonstrate "the Middle Path" of The Infinite Way.

Because all spiritual teachings, and many mental teachings use the same language—the same words, God, Christ, Truth, Spirit, prayer, many students have not found the pearl in the message. Because

37

meditation is not easily achieved, many have given but lipservice to this great attainment. Now we must awaken! We must rouse ourselves to the understanding that regardless of what we have done heretofore, and no matter how much we have studied, meditated, or practiced, we have but prepared the soil of consciousness for the planting of the Word of Truth. This planting *we* must do—so that God, Truth, may give the increase.

As a first step, I urge that students read and reread as many of the Writings as possible; that they hear again and again the Recordings available to them; and that they hold themselves attuned inwardly that the Word be revealed. In the work of 1955—the Kailua Series of recordings, the Monthly Letters, the Chicago and Seattle Special Classes—the way has been prepared for the coming year. In 1956, the monthly Letters, class work, and in the new Writings that will appear (including the new American and British editions of *The Infinite Way*) the Word will become clearer and clearer, thereby leading to the point of realization.

Remember this always—it is not sufficient merely to turn to God for physical healings, for greater supply, home, companionship, or other forms of good. This is but a preliminary step, often necessary to placing our feet on the spiritual path of life. In our earliest days of study it is well if we discover a God at hand, available in all our human affairs, ever ready to heal, save, reform, and enrich. However, this is but the infant stage of spiritual unfoldment. Most of us have been spiritual infants, and some have remained so. Others have advanced to spiritual youth and have found an inner communion with God, have discovered the actual presence and power of God. Through meditation, many have maintained a constant intimate relationship with God. Most people can remember the happiness and pleasures of human youth, but that can not be compared to the glorious youth in the spiritual kingdom.

Out of all the world there are relatively few who have been born into spiritual infancy. The orthodox religious world is just becoming aware that there is such a realm as a spiritual kingdom on earth, and it is providing new spiritual infants. Most of the metaphysical world is still in its spiritual infancy. The Infinite Way begins our spiritual life as a youth, and leads us to maturity in Spirit. Those who come into the realm of The Infinite Way will be led from infancy to youth, and then, through spiritual unfoldment, to maturity.

In two years, divine Grace has carried me to Europe three times—twice around the world, including a great and grand experience which carried me six thousand miles from North to South Africa, and more thousands of miles to Central and East Africa. God's grace has enabled me to speak the Word in the United States, Canada, England, Scotland, Holland, Sweden, Germany, Switzerland, and Africa, and finally, to carry it to India. God's grace has given us American and British editions of the Writings, as well as translations in Dutch, German, and Braille. Imagine! All this in just twenty-four months! God's grace has prepared every step of The Infinite Way, has blessed and prospered its activity, and provided receptivity to its message.

God's grace has been the source of 1955's year of preparation; at every step the Voice has been in my ear with directions for each day, and assurance of what lies ahead. Indeed, in the spread of The Infinite Way we have witnessed the proof of the message. Think you that anything but the grace of God has done this?

Let us see now what things God's grace has prepared for us in these coming years, which are so important in carrying the orthodox world into metaphysical infancy, and developing the infants into spiritual youths. To those who have been faithful to themselves in study, meditation, and practice, this should be a year of great spiritual realization. The time is ripe for those students of The Infinite Way who have attained a measure of youth, to attain maturity—*and that time is now!* Prepare—be alert— the grace of God will carry you through to fruition.

*　　　*　　　*

Out of this work throughout the world have come sizeable groups of students who are ready for the healing work—and this, as you know, is the foundation upon which The Infinite Way builds. Why is healing so important to us? It is not merely because of the physical harmonies which result, for often these are but "loaves and fishes"—but that spiritual healing is the natural and inevitable result of conscious union with God, the fruitage of conscious oneness with our Source, and the direct evidence that what we are attaining is Truth Itself. Those who learn the principle of The Infinite Way, which, of course, must include the understanding of the nature of error, will be healed, and will heal others. It is not a difficult matter—this spiritual realization which reveals harmony where discord has been in evidence—but it requires a consecration to the study and practice until a consciousness of one power is attained.

Here, of course, is the reason that The Infinite Way can bring tremendous spiritual harmony, wholeness, and completeness into manifestation: the unfoldment of the nature of error reveals the awareness of one Power, and establishes us in it. Without this, even metaphysical healing or so-called spiritual healing methods cannot be fully effective, since it leaves the world with two powers, even while claiming one. Happily, quite a number of our students throughout the world have caught this vision of the nature of error, and of the nature of life lived in the acceptance and realization of one Power.

More and more the message of The Infinite Way is being received and welcomed by leaders of other metaphysical and spiritual groups. The wholehearted sharing between these teachers and our Infinite Way work will hasten the day when workers in the spiritual and metaphysical fields will be united in love and truth. Into this consciousness nothing will enter to defile—and from this consciousness, healing will reach the students of all teachers and teachings. When John informed the Master that he had forbad one who was healing because he was not one of his followers, Jesus answered: "Forbid him not: for he that is not against us is for us." Someday, all who are engaged in either metaphysical or spiritual healing and teaching activities must unite in consciousness. Each may maintain his own identity or organized or unorganized form, and yet conjoin in spiritual friendship and in healing consciousness.

Once the subject of cosmic law is understood, all barriers of separation in the spiritual fields will fall away. This we have already experienced in England, Holland, South Africa, and with a few of the teachers in the United States; and now we have received our first welcome in India. I wonder if you glimpse how this "chain of spiritual understanding" —this bond of spiritual fellowship and this band of spiritual consciousness—is extending around the globe? It is important that you understand its significance.

The message of The Infinite Way is finding wide acceptance. Many must be blessed in spiritual unfoldment and more harmonious daily experience, since only the spiritual fruitage of our students is responsible for this mighty flow of the Word around the globe and into foreign languages. With this realization must come a further awareness of the need for more students to accept the responsibility for doing healing work and conducting Tape Recording Work in their communities. While we can be deeply grateful that in many cities now there are students willing to be active in healing, you can readily see that many more are needed.

You are capable of doing healing work, since you have come to the realization that, actually, there is nothing, and no one, to heal; that healing work is but the realization of this truth, in one way or another. You do not, and cannot, heal! *Nor can God!* With this understanding for your basis, it is inevitable that *all forms of discord must evaporate as they are touched by your consciousness of this great truth!*

You know that Truth does not overcome error, that God does not heal disease, that there is no great power overcoming or destroying negative powers. You now understand the meaning of oneness: one Power—without an opponent; one Being—and none human; one Law—and that, Spirit. This constitutes your healing consciousness. Is this clear to you? Then—be about the Father's business, so that you too can say: "Go and shew John again those things which we do hear and see: The blind receive their sight, and the lame walk, the lepers are cleansed, and the deaf hear, the dead are raised up, and the poor have the gospel preached to them."

It is our joy that you receive healing and instruction; that you can smile at the very thought of a presence or law other than God; that the *appearances* of sin, lack, disease, and death are evaporating in your presence. It is our satisfaction when you, in turn, heal and impart. The sick are healed, "not by might nor by power," but *by knowing this truth of One!* Think what will happen, first in your world, and then in the world's world, when *all of us* more thoroughly realize one Power, one Cause, one Law, one Activity, one Being!

Spiritual Guidance

When the eleven disciples were choosing a successor to Judas, they were undecided as to which of two men should be accepted. They turned to God, who had been revealed to them, and prayed: "Thou,

43

Lord, which knowest the hearts of all men, shew whether of these two thou hast chosen." We do not always remember that just as God was able to reveal His choice to the disciples, so can God reveal the men best fitted to lead us in national government and world affairs of today. As we look to national matters, and then to matters concerning the world, let us not be too quick to judge and condemn, but let us turn within, that those whom "thou hast chosen" be revealed, and in such choice the affairs of men and nations will become harmonious.

If we look to God for healing of the body and the mind, if we look to God as the source of our supply, surely we can look to God for things much more important than our personal health and well-being, and that is the health, well-being, and prosperity of all nations and all mankind.

It is much more important that this world be endowed from on High with those capable of spiritual growth, wise and intelligent government, than that you and I work out our little individual affairs. In the working-out of the world's greater problems, our individual affairs soon fall into line, because it is only in the good of others that our own good can be found. It is far more important to pray for harmony and supply for the world than it is for ourselves, but in so doing we find our own good is included in that of the world. Let us find our good in the universal good: therefore, let us pray for ourselves by praying for the government of man by God; let us pray for our supply by praying for the supply of all nations.

Only if we are living in the realization of Him who is our God is this teaching practical; only if we know that God is the Soul of man—a God of love, ever present, ever available, ever pouring Itself out to us as we look to the Father's house instead of to the husks of men.

*   *   *

HOLIDAY IN AFRICA

by

A Student

Imagine 75,000,000 gallons of water rushing every minute over a width of 1,860 yards into a gorge 355 feet below. This is the breath-taking experience known as the Victoria Falls, in South Africa.

A few weeks ago it was my privilege to visit the Victoria Falls with Joel Goldsmith.

Joel had a wonderful time—his winged feet have taken him to most parts of the globe for many years, but here, for the first time in his life, he decided to try being just another tourist. Joel had not only brought a camera, but with it every conceivable attachment and contraption that has ever been devised. He photographed monkeys, baboons, crocodiles, hippos, Barotse natives, falls, gorges, and the numerous islands covered with luxuriant tropical vegetation; in fact, everything in sight, with ordinary lenses, telescopic lenses, 3-D lenses, requiring minute adjustments, it seemed, to every part of the camera. His enthusiasm knew no bounds—every time a spool was completed we dashed up to the post office to mail it away to Hawaii, to ensure that the results of his newly uncovered art would be awaiting his arrival back home. I am sure that as the years go by, and Joel's winged feet again take him around the world, many thousands of his Infinite Way students will be privileged to see these photographs.

On one perfect morning we took the launch trip to Kandahar Island, some eight miles up the fabulous Zambesi River; and on another afternoon, after a long hike in the baking sun, at some remote part of the river we climbed into a red canoe manned by three husky Barotses, and were paddled across to Livingstone Island where, on November 16, 1855, the Falls were discovered by Dr. David Livingstone, the intrepid missionary-explorer—the first white man to see this amazing masterpiece of Nature.

It might interest those on the Way to learn that the Barotse Tribe constitutes about one-sixth of the population of Northern Rhodesia, and they occupy over 350 miles of the Zambesi River. They are essentially a lazy tribe, preferring to bask in the tropical sun and watch their wives carry the crops. However, as they are born and bred on their beloved Zambesi, they are really excellent boatmen. This has always stood them in good stead against potential invaders, just as it stood Joel and me in good stead on that canoe ride at the top of the Falls. History tells us that the Kumalo Tribe of Zulus, under the leadership of the mighty warrior-general, Mzilikatze, broke away from Tsaka and his Impi warriors, making their way northwards to what is now known as Matabeleland, the western portion of Southern Rhodesia. On two occasions Mzilikatze sent his warriors northward, and each time they were defeated in a river battle on the Zambesi by the skill of the Barotse boatmen. For this reason the Zulu influence, which is predominant in the south, never spread beyond the Zambesi.

No story of the Victoria Falls would be complete without a description of the miniature railways which take visitors to the Devil's Cataract, the Rain Forests, and the bridge and back. These cars are virtually two benches, back to back, seating five a side, on wheels with a hood overhead. The locomotion consists of three Barotses pushing from behind, one of whom turns a wheel which operates the brakes.

Some American tourists whom we met on the launch and at coffee at the hotel, remarked at the airport that they felt conscious that something wonderful was happening when they saw us together, but they frankly admitted that they were completely puzzled. I suggested that when they arrive back in New York and read *The Infinite Way* and when they see the line about "golden chains", at the bottom of page 40, they think back to the conversation at the Livingstone Airport. This they promised to do.

I expected to be lonely when I said goodbye to Joel, and for a moment or two the empty chair in the dining-room was quite unsettling. But the feeling soon passed over with the realization that this was infinitely more than just a man that I had been privileged to be associated with—this was a powerful presence, and with that click the loneliness passed away, just as the illusion of error dissolves before the light of Truth. Joel was on his way to Nairobi;

47

Bombay, India; and Honolulu; but something far too wonderful for mortal mind to pen was right there with me.

Perhaps I wrote this merely to assure those on the Way that something very vital will stir in their consciousness when they meet Joel.

CHAPTER THREE

THE PART WE PLAY

Now after the death of Moses the servant of the Lord it came to pass, that the Lord spake unto Joshua, the son of Nun, Moses' minister, saying, Moses my servant is dead; now therefore arise, go over this Jordan, thou, and all this people, unto the land which I do give to them, even to the children of Israel. Every place that the sole of your foot shall tread upon, that have I given unto you, as I said unto Moses. From the wilderness and this Lebanon even unto the great river, the river Euphrates, all the land of the Hittites, and unto the great sea toward the going down of the sun, shall be your coast. There shall not any man be able to stand before thee all the days of thy life: as I was with Moses, so I will be with thee: I will not fail thee, nor forsake thee. Be strong and of a good courage: for unto this people shalt thou divide for an inheritance the land, which I sware unto their fathers to give them. Only be thou strong and very courageous, that thou mayest observe to do according to all the law, which Moses my servant commanded thee: turn not from it to the right hand or to the left, that thou mayest prosper whithersoever thou goest. This book of the law shall not depart out of thy mouth; but thou shalt meditate therein day and night, that thou mayest observe to do according to all that is written therein: for then thou shalt make thy way prosperous, and then thou shalt have good success. Have not I commanded thee? Be strong and of a good courage; be not afraid, neither be thou dismayed: for the Lord thy God is with thee whithersoever thou goest.

Joshua 1:1-9

Not only are these passages from Joshua a continuous assurance and reassurance of the omnipresence of God, Truth, they are also an admonition "to do according to all the law"—to remain in the realization of the Truth—with the promise that as long as we abide in the Truth, turning neither to the right nor to the left, "I will be with thee: I will not fail thee, nor forsake thee."

In order to avail ourselves of spiritual guidance so that we may live under the shadow of this eternal protection, we have a two-fold part to play: we are called upon to be strong and very courageous, and to abide confidently in the Truth. Thrice we are cautioned to "Be strong and of a good courage," as if there exists a great possibility of weakness and doubt. And it is true—time and again we have proven weak and of little courage; time and again we have lost faith and confidence in the omnipresence of God. Over and above striving to be upright and good and just in our humanhood, we must abide in the Law, abide in the Word, live and move and have our being in the consciousness of the Truth. And in order to do this, two things are necessary: "Be strong and of a good courage," and "do according to all the law."

Ho, every one that thirsteth, come ye to the waters, and he that hath no money; come ye, buy, and eat; yea, come, buy wine and milk without money and without price. Wherefore do ye spend money for that which is not bread? and your labor for that which satisfieth not? hearken diligently unto me, and eat ye that which is good, and let your soul delight itself in fatness. Incline your ear, and come unto me: hear, and your soul shall live; and I will make an everlasting covenant with you, even the sure mercies of David. Behold, I have given him for a witness to the people, a leader and commander to the people. Behold, thou shalt call a nation that thou knowest not, and nations that knew not thee shall run unto thee because of the Lord thy God, and for the Holy One of Israel; for he hath glorified thee. Seek ye the Lord while he may be found, call ye upon him while he is near: Let the wicked forsake his way, and the unrighteous man his thoughts: and let him return unto the Lord, and he will have mercy upon him; and to our God, for he will abundantly pardon. For my thoughts are not your thoughts, neither are your ways my ways, saith the Lord. For as the heavens are higher than the earth, so are my ways higher than your ways, and my thoughts than your thoughts. For as the rain cometh down, and the snow from heaven, and returneth not thither, but watereth the earth, and maketh it bring forth and bud, that it may give seed to the sower, and bread to the eater: So shall my word be that goeth forth out of my mouth: it shall not return unto me void, but it shall accomplish that which I please, and it shall prosper in the thing whereto I sent it. For ye shall go out with joy, and be led forth with peace: the mountains and the hills shall break forth before you into singing, and all the trees of the field shall clap their hands. Instead of the thorn shall come up the fir tree, and instead of the brier shall come up the myrtle tree; and it shall be to the Lord for a name, for an everlasting sign that shall not be cut off.

Isaiah 55

Herein we are told that we shall be given an everlasting covenant, an everlasting sign, just as in the reading from Joshua we are assured of the constancy of God's presence. The great prophet Isaiah cautions against living solely for the gratification of human and material comfort and well-being by asking: Why do you spend money and effort for that which does not satisfy? Why give yourself to anything other than that which represents the true Bread; that which represents the true labor and effort for the Spirit? Why spend yourselves for that which does not bring a spiritual return?

We who are gathered together on the spiritual path have come for the express purpose of spending ourselves, our money, our labor, and our effort for the attainment of spiritual realization. As we give thought to the things of the Spirit, by no means do we give up the material comforts of life and the blessings of human relationships; but, whatever we do, we do unto the Lord, ever seeking to acquaint ourselves with Him, for we realize that without the true Bread, these things of the world bring no lasting satisfaction or peace.

We know what we expect and hope of God, but too frequently we do not fully realize our responsibility in bringing about the activity of God in our experience. Even when we affirm and declare truth, we are preparing ourselves for the real experience of inner communion. "Incline your ear, and come unto me: hear, and your soul shall live: and I will make an everlasting covenant with you. . . ." In all endeavors the inner ear must be kept open, alert, receptive, and responsive; and it is this constant listening and hearing, receptivity, and obedience to the Word of Truth that makes the Soul live. "Seek ye the Lord while he may be found, call ye upon him while he is near"—go within, be still, listen, and hear —that is our part in the demonstration. As we listen, in meditation and in prayer, we are seeking God; and it is then that the still, small Voice that goeth forth out of the mouth of God is heard, and then "thou shalt make thy way prosperous, and then thou shalt have good success."

How foolish to be concerned with human thoughts at a time when we should be seeking, listening, hearing only the thoughts of God! But as we open ourselves to God by diligently seeking, it follows "as the rain cometh down, and the snow from heaven, and returneth not thither, but watereth the earth, and maketh it bring forth and bud, . . . So shall my word be that goeth out of my mouth: it shall not return unto me void, but it shall accomplish that which I please, and it shall prosper in the thing whereto I sent it." Just as in the world of nature the rain and snow watereth the earth and maketh it bring forth and bud, so the Word of God, which is imparted in the silence when human thought is stilled, "shall not return void, but it shall accomplish that which I please, and it shall prosper in the thing whereto I sent it."

As we rise to that place in consciousness where we hear the still, small Voice, it performs the activity of healing, comforting, regenerating, and supplying. Once the Word is heard, once the presence of God is experienced, once the inner assurance is received, you may be sure that it does not return void, but prospers in the thing whereto it is sent. All of this happens, however, after we have fulfilled our part in seeking God by turning within; after we have spent our money and labor for the things of the Spirit; after we have listened and heard; after we have communed within our inner being.

It is utterly useless to look for the things of the Spirit to come into your experience except in proportion as you listen and hear, as you obey by keeping your mind stayed on God by acknowledging Him in all your ways, as you pray without ceasing. The presence of God is ever available, but available only in proportion to your individual effort in seeking, calling upon the Lord, listening and communing within your own being; and in that proportion you come to the place in consciousness of hearing the Word. And when the Word of God is heard "in quietness and in confidence . . . ye shall go out with joy, and be led forth with peace." Then it is that the thorns in your pathway shall be removed, and the inharmonies and limitations of humanhood fade into nothingness. This Word will never leave you, nor forsake you;

and "it shall be to the Lord for a name, for an everlasting sign that shall not be cut off"—an everlasting covenant of peace, harmony, and joy—for "the Lord thy God is with thee whithersoever thou goest."

Seek Within

As all students of truth know, God is Love, but do we realize that only God loves, and that all love flows forth from God? You and I are but avenues through which the divine love of God flows, but in many instances we have impeded and hampered its flow to us and from us by the use of the little insignificant word "I." As a rule, we think in terms of "I love" and "my love," and that is where is set up the barrier which curtails the flow.

The realization of God as love is the greatest healing influence in the world, but it bears no relation whatever to my love or your love. My love will not heal you, nor will your love be of any benefit to me; but the love of God, flowing through you and through me, will heal, restore, and reform all within our circle of consciousness, by bringing them into the new dimension of spiritual dominion.

Contrary to the prevailing world idea, your love is not even necessary for the maintenance of your establishment and affairs—it is the love of God; and when the belief enters that it is your love and your effort and care that maintain and sustain your body, business, and home, a sense of lack or limitation is set up. In like manner, it would be fatal if a patient were ever to believe that the understanding of the practitioner was the healing influence, because no practitioner has that much understanding. It is God's understanding, for which the practitioner is but an instrument: the infinite wisdom and divine love of God, flowing through the practitioner, heals, saves, regenerates, and frees.

Erase forever from your consciousness the words I, me, mine, you, he, and she. Realize that only God is Love, and that God loves equally, universally, impersonally, impartially; but, as we have read in scripture, only as we open ourselves to the divine influence are we enabled to receive that Love. Only by actively maintaining ourselves in Truth—spending our money, our effort, our time, our thoughts, on the things of the Spirit—will we ever attain that bread which really satisfies.

There is no such thing in the realm of divine Wisdom as your love or mine: there is only the love of God, flowing to us through each other—the one infinite, divine *life* of the Husbandman, flowing through the vine, the Christ, to *every* branch. No one branch sustains another; but the *vine* sustains every branch, and that only by grace, since it is the Husbandman that sends Its word, Its love, Its wisdom through the vine to the branches.

Regardless of how high in consciousness your teacher or practitioner may have risen, he is merely the vine through which the Husbandman pours forth Its love to the branches. Thus it is with every individual in your experience: he is the branch and you are the vine, the avenue through which the Father, the creative Principle, pours Its love. Remember always this great truth: God is Love, and love is of God, and the vine carries that love, that substance, that healing influence to the branches. In this higher unfoldment of understanding love as being of God, through God, from God, you become a healing influence because, so far as the world is concerned, you are the vine, and all you encounter are the branches; and your contact and conscious union with the Father, attained and maintained by constant turning within, enables the divine substance, the love of the Father, to flow through you to every man, woman, and child, animal, plant, star, and planet within range of your consciousness.

This must be very clear. God is Love. God is the Father, the Husbandman, pouring Itself forth into expression. You are the vine, and all you meet in this world are the branches who are being fed— not from you, not by you, but *through you*, from the Father. This is the love "and the peace of God, which passeth all understanding."

This principle applies also to kindness and benevolence, justice and mercy. It would be a sad situation, indeed, if you were to look for justice in a court of law: but as you look to God, realizing that judge, jury, attorneys, and witnesses are but instruments through which God's justice and rightness flow, justice and rightness will be revealed. Never believe that justice and mercy lie in the realm of man; but, rather, understand that justice, like love, is a quality and an activity of God, and then it is that every individual becomes an instrument through which justice and mercy are brought forth. All the many qualities associated with love— care, protection, security, safety—come directly from

God, and anyone, at any time, may be the instrument through which these qualities and activities flow. As this principle becomes firmly established in consciousness, you learn not to look *at* people, but *through* them, to the Husbandman, the Father, the divine Source; and in so doing you will find that life, in all its outer aspects, changes, and love becomes the motivating force of all your activities.

Meditation

We have been given the caution to look unto God to be saved—to look unto God, not unto man. I am told to repeat this—because evidently a great need is presented here today—there is the feeling that someone is looking to a person, a thing, or a circumstance, instead of looking to God for the good he seeks. It keeps coming to me—"Turn within— Seek Me! Seek diligently *within*—listen for the still, small Voice—*look within for the saving Grace!*" Whatever may be the great need that is being felt here, the word keeps coming—keeps coming—"Seek within yourself! Seek Me—the Lord!" Again it comes—this is a direct message to someone—"Do not look for help to come from man—the saving Grace is to come *from within*, and the contact must be established. Listen! Be alert for the Word that goeth forth out of the mouth of God." Someone is looking outside for help, but that is not the way. Seek within—the help is already established within your own being. Ah!—now I see—it is a problem pertaining to a case at law—and freedom is being sought outside. Freedom is not to be found outside— it is not there! Go within—and realize that the blessing of freedom and release can come only from the kingdon of God within your own being. When the Word of God has been heard within, It will be manifest in your experience!

Seeking Within Reveals the Nature of Prayer

This unfoldment which was given in meditation again brings forth the necessity of understanding that prayer has nothing to do with seeking a person, a condition, or a thing from God. Throughout this entire revelation we are told to turn within, to seek Me, to come unto Me, to listen for the Word. This can be of benefit only if it can make you see what has been wrong with our former understanding of prayer.

Much of our prayer has been devoted to acquainting God with our desires; telling Him what we needed and what conditions we would like corrected or changed. Altogether too frequently it has been an attempt to influence God to do our bidding: whereas, prayer, as we are now beginning to comprehend, is a conscious attunement or at-one-ment with God, so that His blessings may flow unto us.

It is the nature of the sun to express light and warmth. Consequently, when we walk in the sunlight, we have no thought of asking for light and warmth—we merely accept them and enjoy them. The nature of God is love: therefore, there is no need to pray in terms of what we desire to receive from God. Simply entering into the Presence bestows the fullness of Life, Truth, Love—without taking thought, without asking, without praying for them. So think of yourself as walking out into the sunlight, being enfolded in its light and warmth. Think further of entering into communion with God, being enveloped and surrounded by the radiance of the Presence, in which the divine qualities and activities are revealed as the harmonies of your experience. For just as the sun expresses itself as light and warmth, so does God express Itself as harmony, wholeness, completeness, perfection, dominion, power, joy, and peace.

Students, can you not see how we are being led ever higher and higher in the unfoldment of prayer, to that place where, ultimately, we will find ourselves in the very presence of God? The purpose is to elevate us into an attitude and atmosphere of conscious union and attunement, in which we are at one with the Father; into the conscious realization of divine Love, ever enveloping, enfolding, attending us. In this understanding, prayer, and the necessity to pray without ceasing, becomes the most important and joyous part of our lives, does it not?

Let us endeavor to outgrow the belief that prayer is aquainting God with our troubles, or that prayer is asking for blessings of some specific nature. Let us, rather, think of prayer as an attitude of holy communion, in which we rise into the higher atmosphere of Spirit, wherein prayer is recognized to be the Word of God which is to unfold from within. How vastly different is our attitude when all problems are left outside the door, and we turn to God solely for the privilege of sitting at the foot of the Throne, thereby letting the glories of God's grace be unfolded and revealed!

Teaching The Infinite Way to Children

The questions have been asked: What are we to do about teaching this truth to our children? What about Sunday Schools?

I shall answer the last question first. So far as Sunday Schools are concerned, that is an individual matter. Sunday Schools will not solve the problem of teaching, because it is doubtful that anyone can teach a child a principle of life in an hour and expect it to remain with him. Truth cannot be taught in any set period of time: it is a continuous unfoldment and development, and the more one lives in this consciousness, the more will these principles become embodied as consciousness and, ultimately, come forth as demonstration.

If you have accepted the fact that The Infinite Way is a principle of life, who is better qualified to teach your children? Who, in a Sunday School, is equipped to teach the principle that you, individually, have adopted? Truth cannot be taught in an hour or two a week, and, actually, it cannot be taught at all purely in the sense of teaching. Children must be taught much as we ourselves are taught: every time a problem or a need arises, we must apply the truth of being, and this is done not so much in the sense of teaching, but of reminding.

Certainly, you are all desirous that your children and grandchildren grow up with the truth, rather than having to take the hard way forty or fifty years hence. Clearly, the job is up to us if we desire our children to grow into manhood and womanhood with a higher spiritual sense than that of the last few generations, but this cannot be accomplished through our present human teachings, doctrines, and codes. The one way to accomplish this is to start your child where he is now, whether an infant or twelve years of age—start where he is now, and build a consciousness of truth until it becomes a completely natural way of life. It is up to you to build that consciousness, or else let him grow up outside— a prodigal, being something of himself, and then praying to some kind of a divine Providence to get him out of his troubles. That there is no such divine Providence you know from your own experience: the only divine Providence is your individual realization and awareness of the Presence—that is your refuge, your Christ.

The secret of the Christ principle with which we are working is the omnipresence, omnipotence, and omniscience of God. In fact, the entire message of The Infinite Way can be summed up briefly as understanding the infinite nature of God—Its omnipotence, omnipresence, ever-availability. And that is the principle you wish to give your children— a sense of God's presence and power. There is absolutely no way in which that can be built in an hour or two; rather, from morning till night it must be built into the child's consciousness, until it becomes the very fibre of his being.

If you can bring God to a child's conscious remembrance several times a day, either with a sense of gratitude or with a sense of omnipresence, great and wonderful results will follow. An undertaking such as this will entail much patience and persistence. It may be difficult to resist the impulse to say: "Mother will do this for you" or "Daddy can give you that." Instead, turn the child's thought to God as the infinite source of good, by teaching him that God provides all his needs; that God never withholds good; and that God is with him constantly.

Each hour of the day a parent and child must meet some new experience, and the manner in which each situation is handled determines whether or not the child is learning the principle. For instance, suppose he falls and hurts himself. It will be of no benefit, other than comforting him, to say: "Come to Mother, and Mother will make it well." What better opportunity to say: "What's this? You are crying? Can't you close your eyes and feel God's presence with you?" This is where the practice must begin, to make it clear to the child that the Father within his own being is the answer to his hurts.

No child will ever learn this principle unless he is taught meditation. Perhaps you will wonder how it is possible to teach a young child meditation, but it can be done gradually by beginning each day, before the start of any activity, with the gentle reminder: "Let us stop for just a moment, and realize that God is with us today, and that He is holding our hand." That is enough, because the child has been reminded to think of God as an active Presence and Power. A child might learn this on Sunday morning, but by Monday morning that thought is far from his mind, and again it must be brought to conscious remembrance.

There are innumerable opportunities for such promptings. As you set his food before him, remind him to stop for a second of gratitude—"Thank you, Father, for providing our daily food." This need not be said audibly: instead, and perhaps a better way, is to teach the child to say and think inwardly, "Thank you, Father." Before he runs out to play, gently prompt him: "Wait just a minute—have you stopped to let God take your hand?" At nap and bed-time he should never be permitted to drop off to sleep without the conscious remembrance of God as omnipresent in one form or another; and this is also a good opportunity to instill the idea of opening himself to God whenever he awakens during the night and the first thing in the morning. If it is possible to teach the child that the divine Father is always present to provide for all his needs, he will have taken a great step forward.

One of the most difficult things for parents to overcome is the tendency to say, for example: "You must eat this because it is good for you." Often this has seemed the best way of cramming down unwanted food, but now we are going to do an about-face: we are not even going to agree that it is good for him. If we, ourselves, have come to the conviction that nothing is good but God, certainly we must get over the idea of forcing a child to eat this or do that because it is good for him.

Begin now to teach him to acknowledge God every time he eats a morsel or drinks a drop. Never permit him to leave the house without hesitating for a moment to say: "Thank you, Father, Thou art with me"—always being sure however that the thought of danger is not brought to his mind, but just a simple, "Thank you, Father, for Thy presence." Before he falls asleep, let him again acknowledge the Presence with the thought of gratitude that his

Father-Mother God is with him always, whether asleep or awake. Day in and day out, direct his thought toward God, until God within becomes the prime reality of his consciousness. We, who have been students for many years, would not be able to accomplish much in the way of Christ consciousness if we did not live with it from morning till night: therefore, you can well understand the importance and necessity of continually building this truth into the child's consciousness, until such a time as it becomes his normal and natural way of life. After a year or so, you will find that he will acknowledge God as his Father-Mother, and the source of his good; that God has become his constant companion, and wherever he goes, God will walk beside him.

Do not wait until your child is twenty years of age before teaching him that the kingdom of God is within his own being, and that it is unnecessary and futile to pray to a God in heaven. Start at the very beginning of his life to teach the habit of gratitude, of love, of acknowledging the Presence—implanting in his mind and heart the thought that his relationship to God is a sacred and secret one—just between God and himself. Impress upon him that his gratitude and acknowledgment must be spoken secretly and silently, and never openly or outwardly where he might be robbed of his treasure. Many a child has lost his treasure by making his religion public where it is often held up to ridicule and shame. No one has the right to parade his religious beliefs before others: instead, we must go into the secret place, into the inner sanctuary of the temple of our being and pray in secret and in silence—there, away from the thoughts and things of the world, we hold communion with God.

This, of course, does not mean that we are not to offer a cup of cold water when the occasion arises. Offer the cup, but offer it in a way that does not flaunt your religion or give someone opportunity to tread upon it. It is difficult enough for adults when friends and relatives think they are somewhat mentally deranged because they actually rely upon God, so think how much more difficult it would be for a child to have his innermost faith taunted and laughed at by unthinking persons. He is not prepared for that, because he has not yet arrived at the place of an unshakable inner conviction. It is vitally important that his religion be in secret—something which he holds and treasures within his own being; and you may be assured that whatever he learns from the Father-Mother God within himself will be made manifest in his experience.

Children, even the very tiniest ones, should become acquainted with God, and with the kingdom of God within their own individual beings. There is no prescribed formula or set of rules, no rote, no ritual—each situation must be handled in an individual manner, and your own divine wisdom will guide and direct you what to do and say under any circumstance. The main point to observe is to make God a living reality, so that after a few years of such teaching and training the child will have attained a measure of the consciousness toward which you have been building through your own years of study and practice. If children are enabled to come into an early realization of God, Omnipresence, as the mainstay of their lives, it will not be necessary for them to go through all the things that we, their parents and friends, have experienced. There will arise a generation of young people who, from infancy, have learned to trust God—and not only trust It, but rely on It and prove It! Then there will be an opportunity for world peace, because these young people who have attained a measure of Christ consciousness will have no thought of enmity or hatred or envy in their hearts, and their lives will be devoted to giving and sharing and helping, rather than to acquiring.

In the next few chapters, there will appear a series of lessons written especially for children. These lessons, together with the suggestions given here, will be of immeasurable help in presenting the subject of God to your children. If you are able to instill in them the consciousness of the omnipresence of God, you will have given your children the greatest gift a parent can offer—the gift of Life, Truth, Love.

Across the Desk

As more and more opportunities for presenting the message are received, it is wonderful to observe how people the world over are taking The Infinite Way to their bosom and welcoming us into their lives. Recently, in many cities throughout the world, there has been inaugurated a program whereby each student devotes one meditation period each day to conscious realization of the activity of the Christ in individual and collective consciousness. In this way, eventually, our students will form a ring of conscious Christ realization around the globe. Do you understand why this work has been given to us, and what it will accomplish?

You have read and heard that Christ, the Spirit of God in men, will save, heal, redeem, forgive, enrich, make free. And yet, the world remains in slavery to material sense! Why is this so? The secret is this: only the *realized Christ* breaks the bondage to mental, physical, moral, and economic conditions. The Christ, Tao, Brahm, Emmanuel, is always present, filling all consciousness, but—*the fruitage comes only through realization!*

Do you know why so many metaphysical treatments bring little or no healing? Do you know why so many prayers remain unanswered? It is because these treatments and prayers are entirely in the mental realm—intellectually stated or thought— and they have little or no power until an inner "click" or realization, or awareness or release takes place in consciousness. This realized Christ then appears as peace, harmony, and perfection in your individual experience and in the experience of the world at large.

Our work, in every village, city, state, and country where there is an Infinite Way student, is to devote one daily meditation period to the acknowledgment of Emmanuel, the Christ, as omnipresent, omnipotent, omniscient—active in consciousness, individual and collective; breaking the mesmerism of world belief and race consciousness; then, waiting in quietness and in confidence until the "click" or realization takes place. Through consecrated devotion to this practice the history of the world will change.

Gradually, our "golden chain of spiritual understanding" is encircling the globe, and somehow I feel that this time world peace will not escape us—and the spiritual consciousness of those uniting in daily meditation will be the means of its achievement.

*   *   *

ONENESS

by

A Student

The Master, Christ Jesus, said: "Believest thou not that I am in the Father, and the Father in me? . . . I and my Father are one. . . . The Son can do nothing of himself, but what he seeth the Father do: for what things soever he doeth, these also doeth the Son likewise."

Just as the ocean is the essence of its waves, so your consciousness is the essence of your experience. The ocean is salty: therefore, the waves are salty. In the understanding that the ocean and the waves are of one essence, one is enabled to say, "I and my Father are one (of one essence)—yet the Father (the ocean) is greater than the wave (the Son). The wave (the Son) of itself can do nothing: it is the Father (the ocean) that doeth the works. If the Father is eternal, the Son must be eternal, for what power could ever separate the wave from the ocean, or the love of the Father from the Son? "Son, thou art ever with me, and all that I have is thine." If the essence, the Father, is Love, Intelligence, Spirit, the Son must be of the same essence.

Right where the wave is, the ocean is. Consciousness appears as waves—waves of infinite form and variety, such as people, trees, mountains, rivers, animals, etc. In our ignorance, we believe that we can separate the waves from the consciousness that formed them, and give them entity and identity by judging some good, some evil, some sick, some well—while, in reality, the only true Being is one ocean of consciousness, showing forth Its characteristics through each wave.

In our erroneous state of consciousness, we single out one wave and say, "This is I," and our lives are spent busily attending to its wants and desires, until, finally, it passes out of existence by dying. Consciousness is the substance, form, and activity of every wave: and if the consciousness is salty, the wave must be salty, for they are one. Jesus illustrated this when he stated, ". . . he that seeth me seeth him that sent me." All life, love, strength, and activity reside in our consciousness. The wave is but the instrument through which these qualities are expressed, and which shows forth the glory of the consciousness. Each of us must become a beholder of the activity of consciousness—not an isolated wave with a life and mind of its own, but we must realize we are the ocean itself in manifestation.

As we look out upon the ocean with its billowy waves, we are never tempted to give power or activity to the wave. We merely think of it as the activity of the ocean—the whole containing all the waves. If we could look out upon life in the same fashion, we would see all as the activity of God, Consciousness. The moment we think of the small ego, we are separating the wave from the ocean, and delusion is piled upon delusion. We would not pray God to remove the mirage in the desert, or to change the snake into a rope, and yet we pray God to remove sickness, sin, and death, which are just as much of a delusion as the mirage or the snake. Whenever we believe that we are separate waves with qualities of our own, we are in trouble, beset with inharmonies and discords. In singing "Whither shall I go from thy spirit? or whither shall I flee from thy presence? If I ascend up into heaven, thou art there: if I make my bed in hell, behold, thou art there," the Psalmist realized that regardless of the human appearances of heaven or hell, the wave could never be separated from the ocean—the consciousness that formed it. When the Master taught, "Be ye therefore perfect, even as your Father which is in heaven is perfect," he knew that the wave was as perfect as the ocean. There is only one Being, God, appearing in infinite form and variety, and It is always the substance and activity of Its expression.

If you think of yourself as a separate wave, having a life and mind of your own, you wear out; your strength becomes exhausted and your life ends in death. But when you, as a wave, know that the ocean is your life, your strength, your being, you are then as eternal as the ocean, and your life, strength, and being are infinite. Jesus did not heal the blind, the leper, the palsied—he simply removed the delusion that made them exist as separate waves—as separate human beings; and he taught that we would remain in the delusion as long as we had a life of our own, a supply of our own, a mind of our own. When you set about to cure and reform the world, you are saying, in effect, that God's universe is not perfect, and you are trying to change or correct the waves. What you think you are doing to the waves, you are doing to God—for God is the allness of each wave.

All bodies and forms that we behold are the waves of consciousness, and wherever there is a wave there is the allness of God, since God, Consciousness, cannot be separated or divided. When we realize God as our consciousness, we behold the perfect activity of Christ consciousness. When we think we have a consciousness of our own, the waves appear to take on the nature and character of this false consciousness, and the essence of the waves is the essence of this false consciousness. This false consciousness places power in effect, calling some effects good, some evil, some sick, some well. We must always remember that the good appearance is as much of a decoy as the bad appearance. Jesus discovered the truth and taught that we must be born anew of the Christ consciousness. Paul said we must die daily to this false consciousness and let Christ consciousness be our only consciousness. And further, Jesus says that if we "bind the strong man" then we must destroy his effects.

We must always remember that we never deal with the waves, whether the waves appear as patients, unemployment, lack, inharmony, etc. The only truth is the truth about God—*God appearing as*——: in other words, we do not have an ocean and waves, but ocean appearing *as* waves. Since there is only one God, there can be but one Being appearing in infinite form; and what is true about one wave is true about all waves, since God is the substance and activity of all form.

No wave can have any qualities of its own: always it is God's love, God's intelligence, God's power, showing through each wave. Giving supposed power to waves, separate and apart from the ocean, is the cause of all delusion. God is all alone in the world. He is the only Being. There is no other entity to oppose or challenge Him. Jesus realized this and admonished us to agree with our adversaries—resist not evil—love our neighbor as ourself. We bear false witness against our neighbor when we call him either a good human being or a bad one, since, actually, he is the Christ of God, and is a spiritual being. Jesus told his disciples not to rejoice that they had power over evil, but to rejoice "because your names are written in heaven"—rejoice that you know your spiritual identity.

Would it affect the ocean if one wave were to give a treatment to another wave? No! Both the patient and the practitioner are false appearances. All that the wave has is given it by Grace; and when we go into an inner stillness we are flooded by Grace, which announces, "This is my beloved Son"—without beginning, without end, since, again, what is true of one wave is true of all waves.

This realization will dispel the illusion instantly if the realization of the truth of being is vivid enough; or we may have to go back into the closet

73

and "shut the door" many times to the material appearances. We must learn to let the ocean take care of the waves without feeling called upon to correct or reform them, because the ocean and the waves are one, whether we give them a treatment or not. We may give ourselves a treatment so that we may be in a more receptive state of consciousness to realize that perfection is the reality of all that exists, but the fact remains that God's universe is the same, both before and after a treatment.

Humanhood is that state of false existence in which we believe we have a consciousness of our own, and it is this consciousness which shows forth the false human picture which Jesus called "this world" and which, in the last months of his ministry, he stated he had overcome. Our true consciousness is Christ consciousness, and until we come to its realization we will be continually tossed back and forth in the illusory sea of human existence.

The Master realized that the discords of the world —sin, sickness, death, etc., existed only as a false appearance, and he realized that the Father of *this* universe was Satan, whom he called a liar and the father of lies, or illusions. This devil, or liar, would make us believe that we have an existence separate and apart from God—an illusory human being who appears to be born, lives a limited existence of sorrows and very few joys, and then dies. The folly of this human existence should bring us to the recognition that with an infinite Good—God—these experiences could never be based on reality. How could a wave be both salty and fresh? How could

God's universe be both good and evil, sick and well? In Genesis, we are cautioned in allegorical style that we must not eat of the tree of good and evil, because the moment we have a tree of opposites, we have a false state of existence. We must lay the axe to the root of that tree!

CHAPTER FOUR

NEITHER GOOD NOR EVIL

The Middle Path

TRUE spiritual living is based on overcoming the self and being reborn of the Spirit—which is what Paul refers to as dying daily. The only devil is the personal self, or ego, which insists upon being considered and catered to; which is easily offended and hurt; fearful one day and joyous the next. In the physical world, and in most religions, both theological and metaphysical, it is deemed sufficient to rid ourselves of the negative aspects by overcoming sin, disease, etc., yet at the same time desiring to cling to all the good aspects—the idea being to cease being a sinful person and become a virtuous one; no longer to be sick but well; to rise above lack into prosperity. This is all very well as far as it goes, but it has no relationship whatsoever to the true spiritual way of life. In the spiritual life, the world is no more good than it is evil, and in the correct apprehension of this is the understanding of what the Master meant when he said: "Why callest thou me good? there is none good but one, that is, God."

Those of us who have embarked on the spiritual path have done so for one purpose: to bring ourselves into alignment with the spiritual laws that have always existed, that exist now, and forever will exist. As an Infinite Way student, you must accept that responsibility and realize that the degree of progress is strictly an individual matter. However, the degree of unfoldment that takes place at a given time is not up to you. Some, by your natures, will achieve more quickly than others; but aside from time, the arduous work is individual acceptance of these spiritual laws, and the subsequent overcoming of the personal self. This you must do for yourself.

Let us assume that a group of students is assembled for the sole purpose of uniting in the Spirit for communion with God, in order that the truth be revealed. Before we entered, this room was a blank—nothingness, in which was no good and no evil. But as we enter we find an atmosphere of love, co-operation, friendship, integrity, joy— *simply because we brought it here!* There is no dissension because each has come in the spirit of love, truth, harmony, peace, joy—in the spirit of sharing —receiving from the Father and not from each other. No one has the idea of benefiting from another, knowing that whatever benefit is to be derived will come from the Father within each individual.

On the other hand, had we brought antagonism, disbelief, self-interest, the desire to get, to benefit and to achieve, a sense of division, tension, and uneasiness would be evident. You can readily see that you are responsible for the attitude that surrounds you. God fills all space, but the presence of God could not prevent dissension if we had come in a controversial mood. God's presence fills this universe, but that does not prevent wars and aggression, simply because the peoples of the world are ignorant of the fact that the kingdom of God is within the individual. The majority are not united for the purpose of God realization but, instead, are submerged in the materialistic world of acquisition and conquest.

The law of God is love—"Love is the fulfilling of the law"—and the responsibility rests upon the individual to come into harmony with this law. Spiritual love has nothing to do with a sense of personal or emotional love. *Spiritual love is the recognition of God as individual being;* concurring that God is the Life, Mind, Soul, and Spirit of individual being. First of all, that means you: you are Self-sufficient; you are complete in the God-Self within your own being, and you do not look outside to any man, any thing, or any condition.

Because you are responsible only for your own demonstration, it is necessary that you know this is the truth about each member of your family and associates. By realizing that each is Self-sufficient in God, you have no further responsibility or concern for another's demonstration—each is free to make his demonstration according to his own light. It is only natural that you will co-operate in every way, but the greatest service of love you can render is in realizing that God is individual being, and that each one is Self-sufficient, Self-maintained, Self-sustained. When the Master said: "I have meat to eat that ye know not of," he was saying that he was sustained by this inner Selfhood. He further taught that this is true of you and me; and as we come to realize this truth for ourselves we realize it for the world.

This is a universal truth, and here and there, one by one our friends and loved ones awaken to their own Self-sufficiency in God.

There are two forms of spiritual love. The first, and by far the most important, is set forth in the Commandment: "Thou shalt love thy neighbor as thyself." As you behold mortality from infancy to old age, from health to death, from saint to sinner, you are obedient to this Commandment only if you realize that God is individual being; only if you realize that God is the Soul, Mind, Spirit, and the Law unto all being. This is the highest form of loving your neighbor as yourself, and it means no interference in another's life.

The second form of love is found in Matthew 25:35-40: "For I was an hungred, and ye gave me meat: I was thirsty, and ye gave me drink: I was a stranger, and ye took me in: Naked, and ye clothed me: I was sick, and ye visited me: I was in prison, and ye came unto me. . . . Verily I say unto you, Inasmuch as ye have done it unto one of the least of these my brethren, ye have done it unto me." There are many opportunities to heal the sick or to assist someone with human forms of good, but this is never done by endeavouring to live their lives for them; but, as we are informed of some temporary need, we have the grace to share and then go on about our business with no sense that we had anything to do with it— because we did not. It is the grace of God that is all sufficiency! The only way to overcome the self is by realizing that no quality of God is personal; and also, by not accepting error as personal. Whatever of good is performed through you is an activity of God,

79

for which you are just the instrument. Whatever of evil is just a temporary falling under the spell of world hypnotism.

*   *   *

Mark well this principle of The Infinite Way: our work is to bring release from the physical sense of the universe; release from the physical sense of health of body or business. This is quite different from the ordinary metaphysical practice of exchanging sickness for health, lack for abundance, loneliness for companionship. Can you not recall how often you have been ill and prayed or treated for health; or have been in lack and desired abundance? Such prayers or treatments sometimes are successful on the level of belief—exchanging one physical condition, discord, for another, harmony—*but they have nothing to do with spiritual regeneration or realizing Christhood!*

Infinite Way practice means neither fearing evil nor desiring good (physicality) but, rather, attaining the realization of God. We recognize neither good nor evil in any effect, appearance, or form—but, rather, that God alone is the reality, the law, substance, and activity of *all form*. This is release from even the good or harmonious physical sense to a realization of spiritual harmony, spiritual peace, spiritual abundance.

Watch this carefully: are you hating, fearing, or loving the form, appearance, or effect? Are you realizing Reality, that is, Cause, as the fact and function of Spirit, Consciousness—supporting, activating, and maintaining the peace and harmony of *all form?* Are you learning to place no labels of good or evil on form—effect? Are you understanding that discords reveal that you are permitting universal belief, or hypnotism, to operate—when, of itself, such belief or hypnotism *has no power or law?*

Until we thoroughly understand that we are to give recognition neither to good nor to evil—but to Spirit alone as above both good and evil—we have not caught the message of The Infinite Way. Until we desire neither good nor evil in effect, and ascribe neither good nor evil to effect, we have not caught the vision. To pray for the opposite of what we have is to pray amiss. To pray for the realization of Spirit, God, is true prayer. It is necessary that we consciously reject the claim that there is power, law, substance, activity in form or effect, and realize God, individual Consciousness, as the only and the all Power governing every form and effect.

As humans, we are attuned to "this world"— good and evil; riches and poverty; virtue and sin; health and sickness; intelligence and stupidity; life and death. Attuned to "this world" we give and receive hate, envy, malice, lust, greed, doubt, fear, lack, and unrest. But as we rise higher we consciously, hourly, attune ourselves to the Spirit, and as we are attuned to the Spirit *only the qualities of spiritual reality flow from us,* and all who come near "feel" the emanation of joy, peace, freedom, and harmony which is our consciousness. Attuned to the Spirit we need not seek any thing, any person, or any condition—all good flows where we are. No conscious thought of getting, receiving, or achieving is necessary. Our only thought is the realization of our Self-sufficiency and Self-completeness in God!

Judge Not According to the Appearance, but Judge Righteous Judgment

One of the most difficult steps in overcoming the personal self is the conviction that we are entitled to retain our opinions and ideas. This is the last stand of the devil-self, because in the spiritual life we are not entitled to our own opinions and theories, nor are we permitted to judge. In part, this is not too difficult because, as students, we have already come to the place of withdrawing judgments of evil. Whereas, the ordinary man loves to assemble all the facts about the other fellow and from these impressions draw his own conclusions, we have arrived at the place where we no longer condemn, and therefore withhold judgment. The other part is much more difficult, however: we understand that we cannot have an opinion and that we can no longer judge; but now we must go further—we cannot even be satisfied or content or pleased with the *good* in the human picture.

It is the degree in which you are able to overlook the good as well as the evil that determines what degree of healing work you are able to do. If you will be satisfied or happy to see a sick person get well, a sinful person become virtuous, a poor one gain wealth, you may as well relinquish forever the hope of attaining any great degree of progress in the spiritual ministry. Spiritual wisdom teaches that *you are spiritual because God is the reality of your being*. The truth of your being is *God*, and you dare

82

not have any opinion other than that! God is neither good nor evil, healthy nor unhealthy, rich nor poor. *God is!* Should a patient report a fever, you cannot jump to the conclusion that it is an evil about which you must do something; nor can you feel relieved and believe it is good when the fever is abated. When there is no longer a reaction to the human good or to the human evil the most difficult step on the spiritual path, the one which ultimately leads to the death of the personal self, has been surmounted.

In looking at person, place, or condition and deciding that this is good and that is evil, you are judging by the human appearances which are always variable and subject to change. Although a physician may make an examination and announce that you are in tip top physical condition, you must not be tempted to rely on that judgment to the extent that you really believe him, because of what might happen tomorrow. You may look over your list of investments and confidently lean back in assurance, and suddenly have the bottom drop out of the market. One day the world is at peace and the next day something in the human scale goes amiss and there is war. If you are judging by appearances by taking undue censure of the evil and undue pleasure in the good, in either case, sooner or later you come into difficulties. But, if you constantly keep before your vision the Infinite Invisible, you are judging righteous judgment. Never can there be any certainty about a good or evil person, thing, or condition "out there" in the human world—but, if your faith, reliance, hope, and expectation are in the conviction that the Infinite Invisible is changeless Spirit, you are judging righteous judgment, and in overlooking the human picture you will find the Infinite Invisible manifesting in your experience.

Judging according to the human concepts of health and age, the ultimate conclusion is disease and infirmity. But in beholding both the infant and the elder in the realization of the nature of the Infinite Invisible, there is gained an understanding of God as the only Life. Immortality is never achieved in the outer—it is within you. The body, of itself, has no capacity: it is but an instrument for your belief or knowledge, whereby you can either show forth every human belief of age or disease or limitation; or, by recognizing the Infinite Invisible as its only capacity and quality, you catch a glimpse of God as the only Being, thus bringing forth the true vision of immortality.

The body can be made a spiritual instrument by realizing that God is its only strength and the measure of its capacity. This was Paul's realization when he said: "I can do all things through Christ which strengtheneth me," by which he meant, I can do all things through Christ, which is my only strength and life. In your own experience, health and abundance can be brought forth by the realization that health and supply are of God. Wisdom, art, music, literature, business ability can be brought forth through the realization that the Christ is your spiritual capacity. It is when one believes that his health is dependent upon the physical body, and that his mental capacities are in proportion to education and experience, that they are limited and finite. In the knowledge and awareness that the

Christ is your only strength, capacity, mind, being, and eternality—the measure of your manhood or womanhood—the entire responsibility for your being is thereby placed in this invisible Selfhood; and in reaching this conviction you soon find yourself rising to greater and higher capacities.

By acknowledging this same Selfhood for your neighbor you are literally loving your neighbor as yourself, and it is this realization that works miracles in his experience. Your responsibility lies not in your human concept of him, but in the recognition of his Christhood; and in so doing, you are dying daily to the personal selfhood, both of yourself and your neighbor. When this has been accomplished, you no longer have a personal reaction toward either the human good or the human evil in the realization of the perfect and complete spiritual Selfhood in Christ.

*   *   *

As this principle begins to take shape in consciousness, it is inevitable that the thought of some particular person or problem will come to mind, and it will be necessary to take a firm stand against the normal reaction that here is an evil that must be corrected. Right here and now you must begin the practice of dying to the personal self by not permitting such reactions. You must rise in consciousness to the place where you no longer feel that help is needed at all—not even from God! How, then, can you help? How can you express love and assistance?

The patient or student may not always understand that, in consciousness, you cannot agree that he needs help, and so, when you are asked for help,

85

graciously consent to give it. When faced with what the world would call evil of any nature, the first thing is to retire within your inner being with the question that if it is neither good nor evil, what is it? There is only one answer: *It is!* Even though the outward appearance of sin, disease, lack, limitation, or death is evident to the human sense, it is not an actual externalized condition—it is but a mental image or suggestion in thought, like the mirage on the desert. Ask yourself if you are seeing the appearance, or that which *is*? In agreeing that it is only an appearance, an illusion, it can be disregarded entirely, because behind that appearance is the truth which eternally *is*! It is necessary to close the eyes to all appearance, judging neither good nor evil—acknowledging only that *it is*, and in this way something rather like a vacuum is created within your being, and into that place of stillness and peace Truth reveals Itself as the harmony unto the situation. Thus you are enabled to understand that "God saw every thing that he had made, and, behold, it was very good."

This is without doubt one of the most difficult lessons on the spiritual path, but once it is mastered there will be no need for any others, because by then you will be entirely dead to the personal self and thoroughly alive in conscious union with God.

Oneness with God

Humanhood is the story of Adam, which, by its very nature, compels us to put labels on appearances by calling some good and some evil. We are inclined to designate this man moral, this one dishonest;

some things beautiful, others distasteful; certain foods as good or bad for one; this is health, that is disease; and as long as we persist in such judgment we are living in the Adamic nature. But in proportion as we no longer sit in judgment the Adamic nature is being overcome, and gradually we are enabled to look through the appearance, becoming ever more and more aware of the omnipresent Christhood.

In this release of the human sense, it is possible to commune with nature and even with animals, thereby coming into a sense of oneness with all life. Those of you who are familiar with the life of Jacob Boehme know of his spiritual experience in which the "spirit suddenly saw through all, and in and by all the creatures, even in herbs and grass, it knew God, who he is, and how he is, and what his will is." In this connection, and further to explain this sense of oneness, we are repeating the unfoldment and meditation which appeared in the July, 1954, monthly *Letter:*

"The ability to commune with God is given us only by Grace—as the gift of God. The gifts of prophecy and divine healing are likewise gifts of the Spirit, and can be realized only in proportion as Grace has quieted the reasoning faculties of the mind.

"Under Grace the being is flooded with light, the body is weightless and without sensation. There is a oneness with all being and with nature, and one is of the very substance and nature of all creation. This is not being a part of nature or even a part of God but, rather, being the very fabric of Life. One feels himself of the essence of the sea, the actual rise and fall of the waves, the ebb and flow of the tides.

"The being flutters in the leaves on the trees, and is the essence and taste of their fruits. The freedom of fish swimming in the depths of the sea is matched only by the gentleness of the swaying breeze, and the beauties of the rocks and stones and corals beneath the waters. All life is *one*!

"Life beneath the waves is as much a family life as between men and women of earth; life is one in the garden in flowers, trees, birds, and insects— even as the family life of human beings. One Life and one Love surge through all as one infinite divine Being. One Soul unites all creation in Its embrace, and is the Life of all creation. This Life is not separate from the life of the atmosphere itself, so there is no life *in* creation—*Life is the Soul of Creation!* Soul is not *in* any being or form of being—nor is Soul separate from being—*for Soul is Being!*

"I am not in the earth or tree or bird: *I am these! I am* the gentle movement of the clouds . . . the brightness of the sun and its movement. *I am* the breeze in the air, the swaying of palm fronds—yet the palm itself. I look out from the stars—but being also the sky, I hold the stars within me. Beneath is world upon world within my embrace—while I look out from these worlds to the stars above. . . . There is no place where I leave off as the life of one, nor begin as the life or mind of another, but *all is one.* I flow through all, in all, as all. *I am* also the flow. *I am* in musical sounds, yet *I am* the sound itself. Of all creation *I am* the essence, the fibre, the fabric, form, and action—the very Mind and the Life."

The mystical life is the life that is consciously one with God, but you are consciously one with God only when you realize that God is your individual being. In this conscious oneness you do not look at person, place, circumstance, or condition with any opinion other than beholding Spirit. In this consciousness there is neither good nor evil—*only God*.

In absolute Consciousness there is no loss of identity: I remain myself and you remain yourself, and yet there is no place where one begins and the other ends. Those who have been instrumental in bringing about healing through spiritual means know that, when you come to a state of complete quiet and inner stillness, there comes a period of peaceful release in which you are aware of being in communion with the spiritual Selfhood—then it is that you have touched the reality of your patient and found that all is well. You are aware that all of life is a continuous communion with God, and you know that beyond all appearance is the infinite, intangible flow of Love that transcends humanhood. This is the realization of true identity—the Christ.

Because no language has been found adequate to express spiritually the union between the individual and the Christ, most writers and many of the illumined saints and seers have been unable to describe this communion except in terms of human love. When individuals find something deeper than the external appearances of the physical and mental, mutual interests, or religion, that relationship can be understood as communion with the Christ. This understanding, sometimes called the Mystic Marriage, or Oneness, is the relationship that should exist in human friendships and marriage. This is accountable for the fact that in spiritual work often there is a strong bond or attachment between student and teacher, between patient and practitioner, in which, until the communion with the Christ rises above the human levels, there exists an inability to express spiritually. However, with the death of the personal selfhood and the birth of the Christ realization there comes an inner ability to sense another's reactions and thoughts, because when the personal sense of "I" has vanished all relationships are so natural, so simple, and so pure that everything is understood without the need of any outward sign or expression. It is in this realization that your conscious oneness with God constitutes your oneness with every spiritual being and idea.

THE INFINITE WAY LESSON FOR CHILDREN

Love

This is the first lesson I have given especially for children, and so I would like to explain the reason the word "Aloha" is so often used.

Aloha is an Hawaiian word, used both in greeting and farewell, but it carries a much deeper meaning than our ordinary Hello, how are you? or Good-bye. When using Aloha as a greeting, we are really saying, "Love greets you," or "I trust that Love is with you." In the same way, Aloha at parting or farewell means, "God speed you," or "God goes with you."

Love is the most important and universal word

in all the world, regardless of language. You have read in the Bible that the beloved disciple, John, said: "God is love." Whenever you think of love in that respect you must remember that Love, God, is finding an outlet through you; and that every time love comes to you, it is the very gift of God. And so for our first lesson in the message of The Infinite Way, I would like to impress upon you a message of Love, and it will never be difficult to understand the meaning of Love if you will memorize the lovely Hawaiian word Aloha, and remember that it means "Love to you—greetings of Love—Love goes with you."

Our lives run very much like a piece of machinery which, of course, requires frequent oiling. The oil in our lives is love, and it is by bringing the love of God into our lives with as ordinary a thing as a little word of greeting that life is made smoother for ourselves and for others. As you become accustomed to that idea, whenever saying Hello, Good morning, or Good evening, actually you will be saying, "I greet you with Love," which really means "God greets you with Love." If you remember the word Aloha every time you say good-bye or good night, you will be saying, in effect, "Love goes with you."

God fills all space. God really is our true Father and Mother. God is All-in-All in our experience but, somehow, God does not come into our lives often enough. This is because we, ourselves, do not admit God into our lives. It is true that God fills all space, but *you must let God into your life* by bringing Him into all your relationships—with parents, teachers, friends, and everyone with whom you have even the least contact. The spirit of Love is with you always, as long as you are opening your minds, your hearts, and your mouths to express and to receive love and kindness and thoughtfulness.

Of course, not everyone is interested in God in quite the same way that we are. Some people think of God simply as something connected with church or Sunday School, and it really never has occurred to them to bring God into their lives as a constant friend and companion. Therefore, it is not necessary to go around talking about God in their presence, but that does not hinder our using the word love in our inner thoughts, nor does it prevent our utilizing every opportunity to express love in many simple and unobtrusive ways every day.

When leaving home for school or play, it is a loving thought to call out, "Aloha, Mother and Dad," thereby reminding them (and yourself) that Love goes with you, and is present with them also. That is why Aloha is such a charming word to use— especially in your silent thoughts—because every time you think Aloha you are thinking of Love— and Love is God. Because of our daily habits, much of the time you can greet your schoolmates and teachers merely with the usual, "Hello," or "Good morning," but at the same time you can see how easy it is to think within yourselves, silently and secretly, "Of course, Aloha—Love!" Your greeting really does not carry much meaning unless inwardly you also think, "Good morning, God shines upon you," or "Good-bye, Love goes with you and greets you wherever you go." There are many times throughout the day when Love, and all the word conveys, can be used in your inner thoughts, as well as in your outer associations.

The Master taught that whatever we say or think or do in secret will be shouted from the housetops—in other words, whatever you think inwardly, that is what people will receive from you and know about you openly. Perhaps you have never before thought of this great truth of life. Perhaps you think it is possible to have secrets from the world, that it is possible to cheat another, to be cruel to an animal or bird, or to be rude and unkind, and no one will know about it. Divine Law teaches that whatever you think in that little secret place within your heart is shouted to all the world. You can prove this in your own experience by noticing that when you have thoughts of love or sharing or giving, everyone is aware of that love; but the moment you are rude, cruel, disobedient, or disrespectful, there is created an atmosphere in which you do not shine too brightly. Actually, a miracle takes place in your life once you let the word Love come into your thought, because every time you think of Love you are thinking of God, even if you never mention His name, *because God is Love!*

Love is the relationship between you and your parents, friends, and teachers, and that love unites us all as one happy and joyous family. God is the cement that holds us together. God is the tie that binds, and *God is Love*. So, you are really experiencing and expressing God when you are experiencing and expressing Love. When you understand that Love is the bond that unites us, you are understanding that *God* is the bond that unites us. Love is God, and so you can see that God is the real relationship between you and all the members of your household and circle of acquaintances.

All the good that comes into your experience really comes from God. Naturally, your parents, sisters and brothers, teachers and friends, all do many wonderful, kind, and helpful things for you—indeed they do! *But it is God's love they are expressing—all this good really comes through the Spirit of God within them!* It is well that you realize this truth: all good comes through Love, therefore it is of God! Then you will understand that you are fed, clothed, protected, and taught through Love. Is it not because of your parents' love that you are provided and cared for? Is it not because of love for your parents that you are obedient, kind, and considerate?

Whenever you say, "Thank you," remember you really are saying, "Thank you, Father, for Love," for whatever has been given is some expression of God—you have been given something of God. Whenever someone expresses gratitude or thanks to you, it is for some bit of God that you have given them. Whenever you receive a birthday or Christmas gift, or even some little gesture of kindness or thoughtfulness, always remember that you are being given Love, and so you are being given God. Everyone who gives is giving something of God. Every time you give to another, you are giving something of God. Whenever you do something to please and help your parents or teachers, it is really Love that prompts you and, in return, it is Love that makes them appreciate and be proud of you.

94

Is this not a beautiful thought to remember? Is it not wonderful to know that all the good, all the gifts, all the care, and all the love that is bestowed by parents, family, teachers, and friends, is a sharing of God with you? And is it not also wonderful to know that whenever you bring something of good into your home, whenever your conduct and progress in school is good, you are bringing a gift of God into your own life and into the lives of others?

In closing this lesson, I leave with you the reminder that *God is Love, and Love is God,* by saying that wonderful word that conveys my love to you and your love to me—Aloha.

Aloha

Aloha means "Farewell,"
Aloha means "Goodbye,"
Aloha means "Until we meet again under
    a sunlit sky,"
Aloha means "I do not want to leave you,"
Aloha means "Forever I'll be true,"
But the best thing that Aloha means
Is "Peace to you."[1]

Across the Desk

There is no way to establish peace on earth except as Christ, Emmanuel, is consciously realized, and the responsibility is yours as much as mine.

You have come to The Infinite Way not only that your personal affairs come into harmony, but that by loving your neighbor as yourself you can help

---

[1] From the Masonic Magazine, *Brotherhood.*

achieve spiritual freedom for all men. Since these monthly letters go only to those who specifically desire them, it is evident that you are all students who know sufficient truth to raise your world from death in sin, sickness, or lack, to the attainment of life, peace, joy, and abundance. And yet, you demonstrate this only in a small measure. Do you know why this is so? Do you understand why so many treatments and prayers achieve so little?

Primarily, it is because, in meditation, you consciously declare, state, or think the truth of God; you specifically know the nature of any form of error to be but suggestion, appearance, or temptation; you actually know that no form of discord has substance, power, or law—and then *you forget to wait*, in quietness and confidence, for that inner assurance and release which inspires you with confidence in God as the only Power, the only Law, the only, only, only Being!

As you take a specific problem—turn completely away from it—do not permit it to enter thought in any way. Declare or think truth about God, God's law, His universe, presence, and power. *Let thought about God unfold within you!* Declare or think all you know of error, of sin, disease, death, lack: Declare or think that *these are but forms of world belief*—race consciousness, mesmeric material thought—the fabric of nothingness. Then wait—quietly, silently, peacefully, and expectantly. Listen for that inner Voice, click, or release. Be expectant of an inner Grace announcing Itself within you. Practice this several times each day and night. Take advantage of every opportunity. Practice it with every problem that is presented, whether your own or another's.

I ask each Infinite Way student to devote at least one meditation period each day to conscious realization of the presence and activity of the Christ—Emmanuel, Tao, Brahm, call it what you will—permeating individual and collective consciousness throughout the world, breaking the mesmerism of material sense and revealing the kingdom of God on earth. If the message of The Infinite Way does not inspire with love for God and man, it fails in its purpose. If we seek our own good, separate and apart from seeking the good of our fellow-man, we fail. As we, individually, realize Christ, a friend, a neighbor, or someone afar off whom we do not even know is awakened to the realization of his own Christhood.

Dear Students, in your prayer work, please remember this: we are not seeking material growth, financial abundance, or numerical increase. Our mission is the realization of Christ—touching individual and collective consciousness, waking it from material sense, and revealing the kingdom of God, here and now! Through our realization of Christ, we are instruments through which this spiritual Impulse destroys mortal sense, and reveals the man whose being is in Christ. This man is spiritually endowed, fed, clothed, prospered—and is eternally alive in God.

After a month or two of this practice, write me of your experiences. Let me help you, through the monthly letters or otherwise, to the attainment of the consciousness necessary to bring peace and harmony into your world. I shall look forward to hearing the fruitage of this work in your experience.

Peace be with us all around the globe.

*　　　*　　　*

The Principle in Healing

The secret of healing is in the term "The Realized Christ" or *"God Realized."* It is important that you know this: it is not God or the Christ that performs the miracles until it becomes God or Christ *realized!* And the way to realization?

Seat yourself in a comfortable chair or lie on your bed and relax. Completely relax mind and body. Feel free. Turn within with the thought, "Speak, Lord, for Thy servant heareth," or "I will listen for Thy Voice." In this relaxed, receptive attitude there is no mental effort, no mental strain. You are not reaching out to God: you are just relaxing, and gently, quietly, peacefully *receiving the Christ;* calmly, confidently *feeling or sensing the Presence;* and in this state of receptivity there is only awareness, gentleness, purity, and peace.

You do not turn to God for any purpose other than that you "might know thee the only true God"; that you may know "My Peace"—"the peace of God which passeth all understanding." Let there be no purpose, no reason, no object, no thought of self— just purity, spiritual purity of purpose; just pure joy, to commune, to tabernacle, secretly, sacredly, confidently, that I may know Thee; that I may rest in Thee; that I may be at home in Thee.

Be at peace and, eventually, the Word will reach you: "Lo, I am with you alway, even unto the end of the world. . . . I will never leave thee, nor forsake thee"—*I am thee!*

*   *   *

The following is a copy of a letter written to a student exactly ten years ago, which even then expressed the fact that many people are seeking God for some purpose other than God realization. I bring it to your attention at this time because it is becoming increasingly important that we rise above the sense of physical and material good and evil to that place where we embark on the journey of The Middle Path—at the end of which there is but one Truth—*God is! Therefore, harmony is!*

Dear Friend—I have an idea that when people went to hear Buddha and Lao-tse give their discourses, it was much like the more recent days when they go to hear some of the modern teachers. They went then, and they go now, to hear about God and to learn truth. It is probable that those who first sought Jesus went on the same mission, but soon the word spread that those who heard the Master came away healed, and this, no doubt, started the multitudes seeking healing rather than God.

As one seeks God, it is natural that discords disappear because God is the one Cause—the Cause of all harmony, peace, and joy. Those who are seeking healing are seeking an effect, and to seek an effect is like trying to have a loaf of bread without first giving consideration to the proper ingredients. Gradually, our attention must be weaned away from seeking effect, to the place where the whole attention is placed on Cause.

On many occasions Jesus noted this seeking of effect rather than Cause, and he had much to say on the subject in such passages as refer to seeking the loaves and fishes, and in telling the rich man to sell all he had, give it away, and follow him. In that most magnetic section of Luke 12:22-32, he reveals the necessity of taking no thought for effect, and directs attention to seeking first the kingdom of God, assuring us that the Father knows our needs before we ask, and that it is His good pleasure to give us the Kingdom.

This is the line of my thought as I sat up nearly all last night, and I am just sharing it with you.

*　　　*　　　*

As pertinent questions come to my desk, and as they are unfolded, I shall try to answer them for your further enlightenment. One such question that appears frequently concerns the matter of baptism and Holy Communion. What is meant by these terms?

Baptism is an experience that takes place in individual consciousness at the time the Holy Ghost, or Spirit of God, is first realized. It is an experience that comes only by the grace of God. Once in a while it may come when there has been no previous preparation by the individual, but this is very rare. Buddha studied, prayed, sacrificed, and searched for twenty-one years before it came. Jesus received it when he was thirty years of age, having been a

student and a seeker from before the age of twelve—
and immediately he received it, his mission began.

It is the grace of God that forces us to study,
pray, read, and hear in preparation for the experience
of baptism. The experience itself is an immersion
in Spirit, a relaxing in the Word. It is a gentle
release from "this world," with the awareness of
"My Kingdom" forever at hand, after which never
again shall one fear the evils of the world, nor
condemn or judge those who trespass. It brings
the realization that the world has only "an arm of
flesh," but with us "is the Lord our God to help us,
and to fight our battles." Compassion and understanding are born in us in place of criticism and
judgment, because now we are enabled to see that
sin is but an ignorance or lack of awareness of the
presence of God.

After the experience of baptism one is alive in
spiritual consciousness, and only then does one
receive the ability to commune with God. Inner
communion is a complete release from "this world,"
followed by the opening of the Soul faculties, whereby one is enabled to commune with God at will.
While, at times, this may be by words or thoughts
going to and from God, in a much greater degree it is
a Holy Communion of silence, in which the presence
of God is felt, imparting Itself to us, and receiving
us within Itself.

While baptism is a once-in-a-lifetime experience,
Communion is frequent, and by consciously and
unceasingly opening oneself to God, it becomes a
continuous one.

CHAPTER FIVE

A BEHOLDER

Wait on the Lord: be of good courage, and he shall strengthen thine heart: wait, I say, on the Lord.

Psalms 27:14

It is good that a man should both hope and quietly wait for the salvation of the Lord.

Lamentations 3:26

Even the youths shall faint and be weary, and the young men shall utterly fall: But they that wait upon the Lord shall renew their strength; they shall mount up with wings as eagles; they shall run, and not be weary, and they shall walk and not faint.

Isaiah 40:30-31

Part One

THESE are but a few of the innumerable passages throughout the Bible that reveal the importance of "waiting on the Lord"; and this is just what The Infinite Way teaches as learning to live the life of a beholder. This, of course, does not mean sitting idly by with folded hands. On the contrary, the more one waits on the Lord, and the more one is a beholder of God working in him, through him, and as him, the more active he becomes. As a beholder, we still plan our days in accordance with what is necessary to do, taking care of those things which require our attention and which lie nearest at hand. We go about our daily lives, managing our households and businesses as usual, but always from the standpoint of waiting upon the Lord, beholding what the Father gives us to do this hour and the next, tomorrow and the day after. For example, if I have lectures and appointments scheduled in advance, I arrange my time so as to be available for this work, but I do not consider what to say or do during these lectures and appointments. That is my opportunity to become a beholder, to wait upon the Lord, to watch what the Father gives me to say or do at each period of the day. As the work for the next day comes to mind, I take the attitude of a beholder, of waiting, of listening for the subject which is to unfold. If nothing seems to come through, I am not concerned: I simply continue to maintain the attitude of expectancy up to the very moment of the lecture, remembering that this is the Father's work, not mine. Students come to hear the Father's Word, not mine: I am merely the messenger or instrument, and together we are beholders. Students come with an air of expectancy, beholding, waiting for the Word that is to be given; and I also am a beholder, waiting, listening for that Word. It may be revealed beforehand, and sometimes it may not be given until the lecture has been in progress for several minutes. There have been times when students actually knew when the Word was received by the change that occurred.

When I am asked when and where the next class

will be given or what my future plans may be, my usual answer is that I do not know. When the Word is given, plans and arrangements are made and not until then. If we stand aside as beholders of the activity of God, the Father leads us step by step; and we must always hold ourselves in such a state of receptivity that we are ready and willing, at a moment's notice, to change any plans we may have made in order to follow the divine plan.

Regardless of the nature of our work, there are duties to be performed and obligations to be met each day, but by being a beholder we discover that there is a divine Power which guides and directs us; that "He performeth the thing that is appointed for me." Much of our trouble arises from that infamous little devil, the word "I": I want to do this; I must do that; I have planned to go there—not realizing that there is another *I*, a divine Presence that would live our lives for us if we but permitted It to do so. This is the state of consciousness achieved by Paul: "I live, yet not I, but Christ liveth in me." It is as if the man Paul were stepping aside, saying, "The Christ is acting in me, through me, and as me. Christ lives my life for me." That is the attitude we maintain as a beholder, and it is almost as if we were saying, "I am not really living my life at all. I am watching the Father live Its life through me."

This is the ideal way of living—the spiritual way, in which we meet with the fewest obstacles and misunderstandings, the least opposition. In this spiritual way of Life there is no I, me, or mine; the little I has not entered the picture. If I speak or act in accordance with my human desires, my words and actions may incur criticism and misunderstanding; but if I wait patiently enough the Father will speak and act through me, and these words and actions always will be understood. "I live, yet not I, but Christ liveth in me." Always there is a Presence, the Infinite Invisible, that goes before us to make the crooked places straight, to perform that which is given us to do, to perfect that which concerneth us. It makes perfect every detail of our experience if only we can resist the temptation to use the word 'I' long enough to give *It* an opportunity to work in and as us. It is only when I do or speak or think that the outcome may be wrong.

Our entire experience of frustration and mistakes comes from our reluctance to wait long enough for the Christ to take over. Most of us are unwilling to wait until the moment in which a decision is necessary, but insist on knowing the answer in advance. We want to know what is around the corner, what is in store for tomorrow, or even what decisions should be made for next year, instead of waiting until the actual moment has arrived and then letting God put the words into our mouth and reveal what action should be taken. Day by day the manna falls; day by day the wisdom, guidance and direction necessary for that day are given. God does not often advise us a week in advance; we receive the direction as we need it. We have acquired the habit of impatience, and instead of waiting for God's decision to be made manifest, we let fear creep in and, then, afraid of the possibly unfortunate effects of indecision, rush in and act on the basis of our own best human judgment.

Each day we are faced with responsibilities and the need for decisions in regard to our households, business, communities, and nations, and each day we must learn to wait on the Lord, to become a beholder, in order that the decision may be God's. We must learn not to place reliance on human judgment or opinion, and always be alert to avoid being swayed by outside influences. Let us learn to make all decisions in the light of the disciple's prayer: "Thou, Lord, which knowest the hearts of all men, shew whether of these two thou hast chosen." This should be our attitude, not merely when choosing or electing a leader, but in handling every detail of our lives. It applies when making a purchase, when deciding whether or not to make a change or move of any kind. Humanly, we have been taught to rely on our best judgment, to consider all sides of a situation, and to decide on the basis of the evidence what we think is the best course of action to pursue; whereas, in spiritual living we do not depend upon our correct evaluation of human situations. No matter how good our judgment may seem, we turn from it to the Father: "Father, show me the way; show me the next step, and when and how to take it."

With patience and practice we develop the consciousness of a beholder, of waiting on the Lord, and this leads us to a miraculous discovery in which we know not only that there is a God, but that It has become the governing factor in our life; It has taken over our experience. How often we have prevented the activity and operation of God in our affairs by not waiting, by not being a beholder, by not standing, as it were, a little to one side of ourselves until we feel the Father taking over. As we develop our spiritual consciousness we find that there *is* a Presence that goes before us to make the crooked places straight. When we make a human decision, very often we find insurmountable obstacles in the way; but when God makes the decision, His presence goes before us and every obstacle is removed, everything necessary to facilitate the undertaking is provided.

Let us make a daily practice of being a beholder: "Father, this is Thy day, the day Thou hast made. I will be glad and rejoice in it. Reveal the work of this day; show me Thy decisions; show me what Thou has chosen; let Thy will alone be the motivating and activating principle of my life." Let us be very patient and wait—wait upon the Lord, and even if the answer seems to come a minute later than necessary the right decision will be made, and in this experience we will have witnessed the miracle of watching God operating in our affairs. When this has become an actual experience, never again shall we know what it is to be without an awareness of God's government, because we shall have discovered that God *does* respond and that God *does* take over.

The Psalmist's deep understanding of God's wisdom, God's government, God's direction caused him to sing: "Surely goodness and mercy shall follow me all the days of my life: and I will dwell in the house of the Lord for ever." Once we have come into the awareness of being led, directed, impelled, and motivated by God, we shall never again be satisfied to make any decision without recourse to spiritual guidance.

Part Two

Let us now take another step forward and carry this attitude into other areas such as morality, supply, strength, life, and health. This requires a relinquishing of the personal sense of wealth, health, and goodness. For instance, the only good is God. As we permit the good of God to manifest Itself in our experience, we become instruments for the goodness of God. We do not claim credit or expect commendation for our goodness because it is not we who are good: God is expressing Its goodness through us. There is only one morality, only one integrity, only one honesty. None of these qualities is a personal possession! Morality, integrity, and honesty are expressed *through* us. There are no states and stages of these qualities; there are no degrees of them. To be ninety-nine percent honest is an anomaly. One is either one-hundred percent honest or else not honest; one is either one-hundred percent moral or else not moral. Integrity *is*, and it is the eternal reality of our Christ identity. "Why callest thou me good? there is none good but one, that is, God."

Health is not of self, but of God; and in that recognition there is not my health nor your health. If we accept this literally, we shall see miracles occur. Health is a quality and an activity of God, the essence and substance of God. To speak of my health and your health would indicate that there are degrees of health, good health and poor health.

In the spiritual way of life this cannot be; it is an utter impossibility: there is only one health and that is God.

Health is of God—God "is the health of my countenance"—therefore my health is infinite; it is omnipresent, omnipotent, Self-created, Self-maintained, and Self-sustained. It is not dependent upon our thoughts nor even upon our treatments: it is dependent upon one thing alone, and that is our recognition of the truth that all health is of God. Our recognition of this truth is the only treatment necessary. That does not imply that we may not give specific treatments at times, but it means that health is not dependent upon treatment. Health is a quality of God, created, maintained, and sustained by God; and God does not require us to help It perform Its function in our experience. As Infinite Way students we are making a transition from the belief that we are responsible for our health; that is, that we are responsible for knowing the truth in the right way, or giving the right treatment, or holding the right thought. Our responsibility is to know the truth that health is not of self; it is of God. If we know that truth, we shall be free of the belief that we can be either healthy or unhealthy.

For those who seek to understand clearly the spiritual sense of life, the chapter "The New Horizon" in *The Infinite Way*, sometimes called "The Practitioner's Chapter," is the most important writing in the entire message. Most people are not so much interested in the spiritual sense of life as they are in enjoying a harmonious physical sense of life. A harmonious physical sense of life is very pleasant and, of course, it is much more comfortable than an inharmonious sense of physical life. But we, as students of The Infinite Way, should not be satisfied merely with a physical sense of health because, regardless of what degree of harmony we may be experiencing today, it all can be changed by tomorrow. We are making the transition, as rapidly as possible, from the physical sense of health to the spiritual sense of health. And with the spiritual sense of health comes the discovery that health is not dependent upon the organs and functions of the body—health is not dependent upon God alone, because it is a quality and an activity of God!

Whatever is necessary in the government of the body is performed as an activity of God. Let us remember this in connection with the food we eat: the food, of itself, has no nourishing value, no substance, no power to sustain or maintain life, but I, the Soul of me, the consciousness of me, impart to it, its substance, its value, and its nourishment. If we make this a conscious realization, we shall soon find that food will have an entirely different effect upon our bodies than it has had heretofore. "He performeth the thing that is appointed for me," and therefore, all activity of the body is performed by that "He" that is within us. We do not have to take thought about it. He performeth it. "The Lord will perfect that which concerneth me."

It must be clear now that health is a quality of God, and because it is of God it is infinite, omnipresent, omnipotent, omniscient, Self-created, Self-sustained, Self-maintained, forever operative here where I am. So, also, God is strength. My body is not strength; my body does not have strength; nor do I have strength. Only *God* is strength, and strength is infinite. God is life. This is God's life; there is no other. The only life we can have is the God-life which is infinite, eternal, and immortal. This is true in every aspect of our experience. Therefore, let us be beholders of God—beholders of God appearing as our health, our wealth, our strength, our life.

Once we learn to give up the sense of personal possession as indicated by the words I, me, mine, we begin to find the real meaning of spiritual living, universal living, impersonal living, harmonious living. God expresses Its harmony through our being. Every phase of harmony, regardless of its name, is a quality, an activity, and a law of God. When we recognize God as the essence of all good, we become instruments for the expression of a universal sense of good.

Part Three

In spite of this clear teaching of God as the source of all good, all health, all life, many of us continue to be faced with discordant conditions. Apparently there is something operating in universal thought, universal consciousness, that is a persistent barrier to harmony. What is it that acts as a deterrent to the harmonious unfoldment of our experience? What is it that prevents our enjoying spiritual well-being? It is on this point that truth students must be most alert, because the world knows nothing of that which is causing it to be sick, sinful, and poor. The student of The Infinite Way has access to that information, but too often he does not understand how to use this knowledge effectively.

Should an accident occur, or should we awaken not feeling well, it would be useless to examine our thought to see wherein we have failed, to ask whether we have been good or bad, whether we have deserved this untoward circumstance, or what wrong thinking we have been doing, because we shall never find the reason there. The error does not lie within us either physically or mentally. Error, every error we experience, is a universal belief. It has nothing to do with you or with me, except insofar as we have accepted it, and by this acceptance permitted it to affect us.

Let us illustrate it in this way: a child who is too young to have either right thoughts or wrong thoughts, and who knows nothing of truth, becomes ill. The foolishness of searching that little one's thoughts to find what terrible sins he has committed, or what wrong thinking he has indulged that would bring on this illness, should be immediately apparent. The child is too pure to behold iniquity. We, in The Infinite Way, begin with the fact that this illness, claim, or belief has nothing to do with the child. The explanation is that a universal, mortal belief in a selfhood apart from God has operated in the child's consciousness to produce the distress. The child, not knowing the truth, and ignorant of the fact that there are such universal beliefs, becomes the victim of them. But the child is not the only victim of these universal beliefs: we are all victims of ignorance. Whatever of a negative or evil nature is taking place in our experience is not due to our sins—it is due to our ignorance. If a man steals, it is because of his ignorance that all that the Father hath is his; that in order to experience abundance he only has to open his consciousness for the inflow. Had he known that, he never would have stolen. Ignorance is the sin, the snare—ignorance, first, of our true identity; and secondly, of the fact that there are world beliefs operating in consciousness which we passively accept.

On one occasion a doctor, who had witnessed several spiritual healings but did not understand how they were accomplished, asked me to explain how Truth healed. In the short time we were together it was impossible to give a complete explanation, but our conversation gave him a clue from which to make further deductions.

"If we were to open the windows and doors this cold afternoon, what would happen?" I asked.

"We would catch cold, of course!" he replied.

"Yes, that is probably true, if that is what we believe. Now, where will we catch cold?"

"Oh, it might be in the head, the lungs, the chest, or the throat."

"Very well. Now, tell me, which of these organs knows that we are sitting in a draft?"

"What is that you are saying?"

I repeated, "Which of these organs knows that we are sitting in a draft? Does the head, or the lungs, or the throat know?"

"Certainly not! How could they know anything?"

"Then, what part of us would know we were sitting in a draft?"

"The mind."

"In that case, we have to catch cold through the mind, do we not?"

"Why, yes. Yes, we do."

"And the body will express it, eh?"

"Yes, it will."

"Of course," I continued, "the body cannot know that we are sitting in a draft, that is certain. If you are convinced of that much, you are beginning to see why some people have come to the conclusion that disease is not physical. It first must come through the mind and then the belief, entertained in the mind consciously or unconsciously, expresses itself in the body. Follow me just a bit further, and let us suppose that we go out into the rain and get our feet wet. That, too, will give us a cold, will it not?"

"Yes."

"Yet the feet do not know they are wet, do they?"

"No."

"Do you think the shoes know that they have something to do with it?"

"Oh!" he said, "I am way ahead of you now. I never heard of anything so stupid as catching cold because our feet are wet when we get them wet in the tub every day. I can see that."

"All right. What else do you see?"

"I see that I can never again catch cold either from sitting in a draft or from getting my feet wet. The whole idea is ridiculous."

As long as that doctor was governed by the belief that sitting in a draft or getting his feet wet could give him a cold he was subject to the effects of that belief; but the moment he realized that neither the feet, the lungs, the throat, nor the head can know anything about the weather, he was free of the belief that certain material conditions cause colds, and this belief no longer operated as a law in his experience. Freedom from future colds came with the understanding that he was not faced with a physical condition but that this was nothing but a belief.

Now, suppose we know nothing about the existence of colds, and yet we have all the symptoms. How can such a thing occur if we are ignorant of the fact that there is a human belief that germs, weather, or drafts cause colds? It is our ignorance that is responsible for our plight. One might counter with the corollary that because of our ignorance we are subject to a billion different things of which we know nothing. We are. Tomorrow and the day after, and the day after that, all manner of things will be happening of which we may have had no previous knowledge, and these will happen because of our ignorance. This does not leave us helpless, however, because the student of The Infinite Way always has available the means of preventing these things from occurring.

As we have seen, there is a universal belief that drafts and changes of weather can produce colds. If we accept that belief, if we believe that climate is a law in our experience, we are under that law. We have believed that there is a mental cause for physical disease, that resentment causes rheumatism, that hate causes cancer, that lust causes consumption. Although these beliefs may be held universally, their universality has nothing to do with their veracity or tenacity, for a belief by one or a belief by a million is still just a belief, and is never a power.

Another widespread belief of which most people are victims is that each year makes us older; that our life span is determined by the passing of time as measured by the calendar. This belief will operate in our experience unless we consciously realize the truth in some such way as follows: "Whereas, formerly I believed that day following day was a law of age, now I understand that it is a belief and only a belief. My life and my body are eternal, governed and maintained by a divine Source which is within me. I, therefore, am no longer affected by the passing of time. The calendar is not a law: it is a belief, and a belief cannot operate in my consciousness as law. Within me is the fullness of life." As this recognition becomes a specific activity of consciousness, the effects of age on the body are nullified.

Now is the time to eliminate such beliefs from consciousness because they are not true and never were true. Once we arrive at the recognition that these beliefs are not laws, are not power, are not cause, we have reached one of the most important moments in our spiritual unfoldment. We are governed either by our consciousness of truth or by our ignorance of truth. Whatever may be the world belief that claims to cause the sin, disease, lack, limitation, or death, it is not cause, it is not power! The knowledge of this fact is our "shield and buckler." Truth students frequently complain: "Despite the fact that I have been in truth for years, I continue to experience disease, poverty, and inharmony. How can this be?" There is only one answer.

They have not been in truth. They have been attending truth centers or reading truth books, but they have not been in truth. No one is ever in truth until he takes the truth into his consciousness and begins to live it. The way to do this is to understand that we are the spiritual offspring of God, and are, therefore, God-governed, God-maintained, and God-sustained. That must be an unshakable conviction within us. To know that God is infinite, and that "I and my Father are one," is the basic principle of The Infinite Way. But this, alone, is not enough. In addition, it is necessary to understand that whatever in human belief claims to cause sin, disease, lack, limitation, and death is but a belief and not a law, is but a theory and not a demonstrated fact. Such understanding begins to dispel the discords from our experience.

Christopher Columbus was one of the few men in the fifteenth century who believed the earth to be a sphere. Most of his contemporaries were convinced that the earth was flat and that the sky and the water met at the horizon. But this one man, in his correct perception of the world as it is, not only was himself no longer in bondage to world belief, but also was instrumental in freeing others from the limitations of this belief. We must recognize that there are universal beliefs which operate in consciousness, even though we may never have heard of them. Theories of materia medica, astrology, or theology, are not laws but beliefs entertained in human thought; and because they are merely beliefs they can only affect the believer. Everybody may believe in sin, disease, lack, limitation, and death, but one enlightened soul, one Christ Jesus, nullifies these beliefs, not only for himself, but for the multitudes. We can be of the ignorant multitudes who live according to material law, or we can be one of the spiritually illumined, who comes out and is separate. We can be the ones to realize: "No longer do these mass beliefs operate in or through my consciousness. My consciousness is a vehicle for God, a channel for Truth. My body is an instrument for the expression of Life, Truth, Love, harmony, wholeness, and perfection. My whole consciousness is alive, alert, awake, receptive, and responsive to Truth. Into it nothing can enter that defileth or maketh a lie. None of these world beliefs, none of the theories of materia medica, astrology, or theology—none of these can enter my consciousness. I understand such ideas to be beliefs and not laws." Universal beliefs are power only to those who accept them, or to those who do not recognize that the cause of their discord is a universal belief accepted as law. The moment we recognize discord for what it is, a universal belief, it cannot operate in our consciousness as cause or as law. Only God and the things and thoughts of God can operate in the consciousness of one who is awake to this truth.

To live as a beholder, we must hold these two important principles always before us:

1. God is infinite, all. "I and my Father are one," and all that the Father hath is mine; and only that which emanates from the Father can, and does, manifest in and through me.

2. Error is a universal belief, a world belief, always without presence or power, or law to sustain it.

In this wisdom, let us recognize all discords as universal belief; let us "wait on the Lord"; let us be beholders of God, guiding, maintaining, and sustaining Its own; God fulfilling Itself as individual being. Then "we shall see him as he is"—God appearing as the wholeness, the abundance, the harmony, the peace, and the joy of our experience.

Peace

It is a beautiful, calm, serene, and peaceful day here in Hawaii, and from my window I look out upon a bright blue sky, filled with lazily moving, fleecy white clouds. Close at hand is the rhythmic sound of the surf, and in the distance the little grey doves can be heard calling softly back and forth. All about there is an atmosphere of Peace, which is the atmosphere of God's love. There can be no doubt about that Love: evidence of it can be seen everywhere, especially in the beautiful colours and varieties of the flowers and foliage. Why, just the other day, I was told that on the Garden Island of Kaui there are five thousand species of one flower, and so you can imagine how many, many colours and forms must appear in just that one plant. Only God's love for His children and for His creation could bring forth such an abundance of beauty of form, color, variety, and fragrance. And so today, as I give you my aloha greeting of love, it comes to my thought that love is another name for peace. Whenever I think of God, I think of love; and whenever I think of love, I think of peace, for God is *Love* and God is *Peace*!

The dictionary defines peace as a state of tranquility or quiet, freedom from fear and conflict, harmony. This definition brings to mind a wonderful and beautiful message from our Master and Teacher, Christ Jesus, wherein he says: "Peace I leave with you, my peace I give unto you: not as the world giveth, give I unto you. Let not your heart be troubled, neither let it be afraid." Jesus always told us that, "My doctrine (that is, Jesus' teaching) is not mine, but his that sent me." In other words, Jesus came to earth to give us God's message, and so when he says, "My peace," he, of course, means God's peace. Every word of the Master is meant to be used for the glorification of God in our experience; every word is meant as a fulfilment of love, of good, to you. When Jesus says, "I am come that they might have life, and that they might have it more abundantly," he was really saying, "I am the Son of God, and I am bringing the love of God to you. God's peace reaches you through me."

This is true in your own experience. Just as Jesus was the Child of God, the Messenger who brought "My peace"—the peace of God to you—so are you young people the children of God who must bring the love of God and the peace of God to your families and friends, and into your homes and schools. You children must accept the same responsibility that our great Teacher accepted, and wherever you go you too must be willing to say, silently and secretly, of course, "I bring the peace of God to this home, to this schoolroom, to this playground. The peace of God in me I bring unto you." There may be an occasion now and then when you may speak this in words, but you will remember what I told you in our first lesson—*you do not have to say it aloud*. For instance, when you come home from school, instead of rushing in helter-skelter, pause for just a little moment and remember that you are bringing peace—"My peace"—the peace of God into your household, and when you do that you bless every member of your family. In the same way, when you enter your classroom or a store, or any other place you may happen to go, remember that *you* now carry with you the peace that the Master gave to you, and always be ready and willing to give it forth to others. In this realization of God's peace, there will be no need for any students to fall back in their studies or fail in their examinations; there need be no unruly, unkind, or thoughtless children; there need be no harsh or impatient teachers. Part of the responsibility for your schoolmates' success and for your teacher's good nature, rests upon *you*!

Up to now, perhaps you have thought that all the responsibility was upon your parents, or your older brothers and sisters or your teachers, but now you must accept some responsibility yourselves. And the first responsibility that you can accept is love. You, as children of God, must bring the same message of love into your circles that the Master brought into his when, in speaking to his disciples, his mother and brothers, he said, "My peace I give unto you." You must bring that same peace into your homes, schools, and playgrounds.

The Master once was asked which of the Commandments was the greatest, and he answered that the first Commandment was to love God with all your heart, with all your soul, and with all your mind; and the second was to love your neighbor as yourself. In order to be an Infinite Way student at all, you must make love the central theme of your whole existence: first, in your love to God, and secondly, in your love to all those with whom you are brought into contact.

There is a systematic and orderly way to do this and, if you are really sincere in being students of The Infinite Way, it is a way which you can practice with very little trouble or effort, and without forgetting. First of all, remember these words of the Master, Christ Jesus: "Peace I leave with you, my peace I give unto you." Memorize these words, learn them by heart—"My peace I give unto you"— and every time you enter or leave your homes or your school just remember, God's peace I leave with you.

Across the Desk

From the articles appearing in the newspapers and magazines, one would believe that there is a spiritual revival in the world; that people the world over are desperately seeking God; that the overflowing churches and increased church memberships indicate this spiritual surge.

Let us not be fooled by this. The greater the church attendance, the less spirituality is shown forth. It is important that you know the facts. If you will ask the question, Why this filling of the churches? you will learn that the pews are not filled with those seeking *to know God*, or seeking *to learn*

God's will, but rather, *to get something from God* that God has not been giving them—presumably because they remained away from church. This is not spirituality, but dense materiality and self-seeking!

And these things that the people seek of God —are they finding them in and through the churches? Are they finding peace? And if so, why the great interest in television, radio, movies, prize fights, and other non-spiritual diversions? Are they finding health? Then why are magazines and papers filled with more and more news of miracle drugs and new discoveries and cures in medicine? Are people finding serenity and sanity? Then why the increasing need for more and larger mental institutions, alcoholic and drug cures, rest homes and sanitoriums? Is crime lessening? Juvenile delinquency? Are the churches answering these problems or meeting them? Are people finding spirituality there? Are people finding God there? The answer is obvious. Then wherein is the failure of the churches to meet the needs of today?

Only in knowing God can we find life eternal! Only in understanding prayer can we achieve freedom from material conditions! The churches neither know, nor can they teach, the nature of God and the nature of prayer. Praying to God for peace, for health, for safety and security is a waste of time. The prayer of the righteous man is a prayer to know and understand and *experience God!* The prayer that availeth much is a prayer in which God's will is asked. The healing prayer is a prayer that God's grace be realized, that God's will be done.

Infinite Way Students! Learn that God cannot

123

be influenced, coerced, bribed, or otherwise prevailed upon to do anything that is not already *being done by Him!* Seek nothing of God but God Himself. Be satisfied with nothing less than the experience of God—the actual awareness of God's presence. Surrender your desires. Give up your wishes. Acknowledge God as the all-knowing spiritual Intelligence. Rest in the truth that *it is God's good pleasure to give you the kingdom.* Relax in the assurance of God's grace. Cease being a beggar. Desist from demanding of God. Call a halt to telling God of your needs. Rest! Relax! Rejoice! In Him we truly live—*then live in Him!* His fullness is our completeness. His perfection is our wholeness. His love is our assurance of grace. Rejoice in His love!

You will know when the world starts on the spiritual path—when the people seek God, instead of things and conditions. You will know when the world begins to pray—when you hear: "Reveal Thyself, O Lord; Speak, Lord, thy servant heareth" —instead of "Listen, Lord, thy servant speaketh," and asketh and beggeth—and sometimes even demandeth!

You will know when *you* have entered the spiritual path, The Infinite Way of life—when you surrender your desires and wishes and hopes, and seek to know God, to meet God face to face, to experience God. You will know that the divine harmonies will flow when you no longer seek harmony, but seek "to know thee, the only true God." When you are weary of seeking demonstrations, your strength will be renewed in Him. When you tire of seeking supply, companionship, employment, you will rest in His grace and find peace, contentment, abundance, freedom, and joy.

* * *

The study of the Gospels will reveal (among other things) three important points worthy of serious consideration:

1. Through consecrated study, meditation, association, application, all may attain a measure of Christ realization. The measure of attainment is dependent upon the depth and degree of consecration and devotion to the achievement.

2. An individual who is imbued with the Christ realization is a law of harmony, peace, health, supply, completeness to those receptive to the spiritual Impulse. Such an individual, attaining Christ realized, dispels the material sense which has produced the good and the evil physical sense of existence, and reveals the spiritual presence of eternal harmony and wholeness.

3. *Only individuals receptive to the spiritual Impulse* (only those having a capacity for Christ) *can benefit.*

On this third point, be careful. It is not our degree of human worthiness, goodness, or virtue that determines our receptivity to the Christ, or our ability to attain God realization. Often the sinner proves as receptive as the human saint. *Christhood is attained only in the measure of our ability to be unselfed.*

CHAPTER SIX

IN GOD'S PRESENCE IS FULLNESS OF LIFE

Part One

IN speaking with the Samaritan woman, the Master said: "Whosoever drinketh of this water shall thirst again: But whosoever drinketh of the water that I shall give him [it] shall be in him a well of water springing up into everlasting life." Later that same day, when the disciples urged him to eat, he answered: "I have meat to eat that ye know not of." On another occasion he said: "I am the way, the truth, and the life: no man cometh unto the Father, but by me." Once we glimpse the profound and sublime truth contained in these mystical utterances, our attitude changes completely and life assumes an entirely different meaning, for then we understand that "Man shall not live by bread alone," but that the "Word that proceedeth out of the mouth of God" is the substance of all life.

As we begin to perceive that that which is outwardly tangible and visible is but the product of that which is invisible, we no longer judge our supply by the size of the purse but by the degree of God-contact attained. In attempting to find the fullness of life without first having made the contact with the Father within, we find ourselves with dust and ashes. It is imperative, therefore, that we gain an awareness of the divine Presence before the fullness can appear in our experience.

Whatever good is to appear in our lives must appear as the result of the activity of truth in our own individual consciousness. If we maintain the same consciousness today as yesterday, we can expect no different fruitage; and in order that our experience tomorrow have a new and different and greater unfoldment, there must be a new activity in consciousness today. In other words, if we are to reap any spiritual fruitage from the study of truth, we must rid ourselves of whatever dead branches we are clinging to. Through a specific activity of consciousness, we must purge ourselves of any false beliefs we have entertained about God or Truth.

As a beginning, we must reconstruct our ideas and concepts of prayer. It is evident that we have entertained a belief that it is possible to pray to God for something and receive it; and so, heretofore, we have prayed in order to gain something or to bring about some desired condition. Now we must consciously renounce such a belief and concept of prayer, and enter into a state of silent meditation in which we consciously remember that since the kingdom of God is within you, no longer need you look outside your own being for anything to come *to* you. Instead, *you must open out a way for it to flow from you!* This is impossible of accomplishment, however, unless you consciously come into the understanding of your own Self-completeness by making the sacrifice of everything of an external nature.

In The Infinite Way, meditation, communion, and

prayer can be rightly defined as "waiting upon the Lord." How we long to stand before the Ark of the Covenant and there experience the presence of God! But before entering the Holy of Holies we must make the sacrifice of all beliefs of a personal or material sense that might be a barrier to this communion. What has held up our spiritual progress heretofore? It is surprising, if we search deeply enough, to find how many universal beliefs we have been holding, and how difficult it is to relinquish them. If you have been depending upon investments, positions, or families for supply, you must consciously withdraw attention from those sources and realize that all good must flow from the infinite Source within your own being. Perhaps you have looked to loved ones or friends for gratitude, understanding, love, and co-operation. Now you must consciously loose these dependencies and expectations and let them go by inwardly realizing that the error lies in looking to any person, situation, or thing for your good. The very first of these that must be abandoned is the belief that any person, any thing, or any condition of the world can provide lasting happiness and security and peace. If we have been looking "out there" for love, supply, or health, these very things have operated as insuperable barriers in our consciousness. As we enter the Temple of our inner being, we must surrender and cast into the sacrificial fire every material and mental obstacle and belief that stands between us and our Heavenly Father.

In this communion we must lay aside even the desire to be helpful and to do good, or to be healers; and, strange as it may seem, we must surrender even the desire to attain Christhood! Surrender everything but the desire to stand before God! Watch this carefully, and be sure you are not secretly harboring a desire for something besides God! We must, literally and actually, mean it when we say "Thy Grace is sufficient for me," and if we are successful in surrendering every desire of a mental, mortal, or material nature it will not be too long before we will stand in the Presence. But remember, we cannot carry our burdens into the Temple, nor can we have any desire that God will do something to lighten them. We will stand in the Presence only when we have been purified of all human desires and hopes in the actual realization that the grace of God really is our sufficiency in all things.

God is not a far-off God, separate and apart from us. No, no, no! God is within us, and He must be consciously realized within us! But this realization will never come to anyone who desires God for any purpose other than the realization itself! Everyone who has sought God for any other reason has missed the way. God can be attained only by a complete surrender of everything but the desire to bask in His presence. It is in the degree that you make this sacrifice within your own consciousness that "Thou shalt decree a thing, and it shall be established unto thee: and the light shall shine upon thy ways." If you will decree this surrender and consciously let go in the realization that life is not lived by bread alone, but by every Word that proceedeth out of the mouth of God, you will soon find that the Christ-peace, the necessary step leading to spiritual fulfilment, will follow.

As we divest ourselves of material and human dependencies, the use of words such as I, you, he, she, and it, will diminish, and we shall not give so much thought to those persons and things from which we formerly expected so much. Now as needs arise, the first thought will be the Christ, and in this awareness whatever is necessary and needful for the fulfilment of your experience will be forthcoming—not from you, him, her, or it, but from the Christ of your own being. It is true, of course, that the Christ sometimes will appear as human avenues or channels. For instance, your good can come through me, and my good can come through you: but my good will not come from you, nor will your good come from me. As we look only to the Christ of our own being, the Christ appears as that which we need. Perhaps today, as you look only to the Christ of your own being, the truth appears as me through these written words, but tomorrow and the next day it will appear as someone or something else—but always it will be the Christ appearing.

As you learn to personalize your good and the avenues of your good less and less by permitting dependencies to fall away and subside, you realize the Christ to be the source and fount of all good, and by continuously looking to the Christ your good will flow. When the Master said, "I am come that they might have life, and that they might have it more abundantly," he was telling us that our families, friends, positions, and bank accounts are not fulfilment, but that I, the Christ of your own being, am your fulfilment. Over and over again in the promises of scripture we are reminded and assured of the presence of God. In every circumstance, in every trial, and in every tribulation, "God is with thee whithersoever thou goest."

Part Two

In Genesis, we read that if ten righteous men were found in the city, the city would be spared. A righteous man is one who has attained conscious oneness with God. Therefore, the sole purpose of meditation is to achieve this state of union or oneness. As you, individually, attain conscious union with God, you become that very Spirit through which God pours Itself; and as you place utter and complete reliance on the Christ, the divine Presence within, you begin to realize that you *are* that place through which God shines upon the world. As you accept this rather earth-shaking realization and are willing to be the instrument or avenue through which good flows out to the world, you make the transition from being a branch to being the vine. Jesus was enabled to feed the multitudes, heal the sick, and raise the dead, only because he had attained conscious union with God; and it will be your conscious union with the Father that will enable you to become the vine, the infinite source through which all the God-head flows—feeding, healing, illuming, saving, and redeeming those branches who do not yet know their Self-completeness in God.

Spiritual man, the Christ, can have no desires. Spiritual man, our true being, simply stands and serves, and rests in his conscious union with the Father. The moment we attain Christhood, by completely discarding all outward reliances, we become the channels through which the infinite, spiritual good of the divine Source flows into visible expression. Can you not readily see the necessity for making the transition from humanhood by dying daily to that part of you that ever had a desire for personal good, and being reborn into the spiritual awareness of the infinite nature of your own being? Knowing your Self-completeness in God, how can you possibly pray for any *thing*? Instead, your prayer is a paean of gratitude: Thank you, Father, I am. All that Thou art, I am. All that Thou hast is mine. I am. Thank you, Father, I am. In this prayer you become aware that that which you have been seeking already is embodied within your own individual being, and that it is only necessary to open wide the gates of consciousness and let it flow into visible expression.

As you begin to perceive the tremendous meaning of this truth, it is only natural that questions come to mind: Am I worthy of this great good? Do I deserve it? Have I sufficient understanding to receive it? Have I time for all the work and study and prayer necessary to come into this realization? In answer to these questions it is important that you know this fact: *Nothing can stay the hand of God!* This good is the pure activity of the Christ, and is not dependent upon anything that you do. Your sins of omission and commission do not act as a barrier to this activity, and nothing you can do or ever have done can prevent it. This realization is not determined by the amount of time devoted to reading, studying, and meditating. These are merely aids to open your consciousness. God is not waiting until you become virtuous or read so many books or meditate so many hours. God is in constant activity—omnipresent, omnipotent, omniscient—and the only requirement on your part is that you open consciousness to receive it.

The Christ is the reality of your being, now!—and It is waiting in abeyance, so to speak, for you to let It in: first, by erasing and discarding all beliefs that God is something separate and apart from your own being; and, secondly, by relaxing and letting It flow forth. You are Self-complete in God. The infinity of God, Good, is flowing forth, much more than you can ever accept; but holding to the belief that this divine Grace is dependent upon what you do or do not do humanly is a barrier to the fullness of Its expression. All truth already is within you, and the work that you do by way of studying, reading, and meditating is not for the purpose of obtaining God's grace, but to enable you to open consciousness to the inflow, thereby drawing Its infinity forth from within your own being. Never, in any way, believe that you can bring about the grace of God or prevent it. It is already full and complete within your own being, awaiting the awareness of your fullness in Christ; awaiting the acknowledgment that the grace of God *is* your sufficiency in all things; awaiting the recognition that the peace of God is all you will ever want or need. In this realization, all that is needful for fulfilment will appear in infinite form and variety in your experience.

This realization of the indwelling Christ is a "Peace, be still" to all forms of discord. Though your sins be as scarlet, they shall be as white as snow. Though you be crucified, today thou shalt be in paradise. Thy sins are forgiven thee, because there is no penalty for that which no longer exists. "Thou art made whole: sin no more, lest a worse thing come unto thee." Now that we know the truth, we will evoke greater trouble if we go back to the old belief of a sense of separation from God that brought us into difficulties in the first place. Go, and sin no more! Never go back to the old ways of seeking your good humanly from person, place, or thing. Loose these old beliefs, and let them go in the realization that you live and move and have your being in God!

Often, when faced with the appearances of discord, pain, lack, and limitation, our first temptation is to make a mental effort to achieve peace or harmony or healing by forcible and strenuous thought-taking in the way of affirmation and denial. This only serves to make us tense. Now we will reverse this, and whenever there is an appearance of discord we will relax in the remembrance that our good does not come by mental might nor physical power, but by the very gentle Spirit within the depths of our own being. We can dismiss any discord in the awareness of the Christ-peace—"Peace I leave with you, my peace I give unto you: not as the world giveth, give I unto you. Let not your heart be troubled, neither let it be afraid." Therefore, we will make no effort to achieve a healing: instead, we will become still and quiet and confident in mind and body so that the Spirit may descend upon us, and that we may hear the still, small Voice. Be still! Why struggle and strive as if it were necessary to search for God and, once finding Him, to cling to Him? Be still! He leads us beside the still waters and into the green pastures wherein we find peace. Be still! Who, by taking thought, can accomplish anything? What clothes the lilies in the field? What guiding Spirit leads the birds to their nesting places? It is the love of God, the grace of God, the sufficiency of God in the midst of each and every individual, but we can receive this fullness only in stillness, in quietness, and in confidence.

Though we be called upon to walk through the valley of the shadow of death, "Thou art with me; thy rod and thy staff they comfort me." Here we understand that it is not our thoughts or words or treatments that comfort and heal, but the presence of God, and so, even in the midst of these seeming discords we can relax and rest in the awareness of God's grace. It is not your mind or your thoughts or your ways that are the healing influence, but the Christ at the center of your being. Why not give up your thoughts and ways and your doubtful mind, and let the still, small Voice assure you that "I will never leave thee nor forsake thee"? As you lean back in the everlasting arms, knowing that you are maintained and sustained by the Word of God, you are enabled to receive of the living waters that spring up into life eternal. It is as if the gentle Christ Itself were speaking: "Fear not. My Spirit is with you. My Presence goes before you. Rest in me. You need not strive for your good, because your Heavenly Father knoweth that you have need of these things, even before you ask, and it is His good pleasure to provide for your every need."

As attention and reliance are withdrawn from the world of persons and things, gradually you become more conscious of the fact that the Word of God is as hidden manna—hidden within the depths of your own being, invisible to the world of sense and humanhood. This is the meat, the bread, the wine that the world knows not; and you can always turn to it in confidence, in peace, and in joy, in the awareness that the kingdom of God is within you, and all that the Father hath is yours. Whenever an appearance of discord looms upon the horizon, be at peace in the assurance of the divine Presence, and let the Christ be the avenue through which you are provided, maintained, sustained, and protected. "Believe ye that I am able to do this?" If your unreserved answer is, "Yea, Lord," you can trust the Christ, whose only function is to bless and be a benediction unto you. As you cease to put your faith in princes and no longer live by bread alone, you will find that every promise of holy scripture is fulfilled in you, for "Thou wilt shew me the path of life: in thy presence is fullness of joy; at thy right hand there are pleasures for evermore."

Faith

Millions of fine people the world over "believe" in God; have "faith" that God will heal, save, reform, enrich—as the case may be. Most of these earnest ones go through an entire life span—believing, having faith—yet witnessing little or no fruitage from their faith. Actually, it has rarely been revealed to the world that faith is not an activity of the mind; is not an act or concept of the intellect—and therefore such believing or faith is without "signs following."

Faith is a spiritual perception entirely apart from .conscious thought or human reason. Faith is a transcendental quality, an act of the Soul. Faith is achieved only as one refuses "to believe" or "have faith" and retires into the withinness of himself, and there asks for light and spiritual realization. Faith is the ability to see the invisible, hear the inaudible, know the unknowable—and this is possible only through inner vision or spiritual perception.

Naturally, here the question arises: Can a person living the normal human life, engaged in family and business pursuits, achieve the faith which moves mountains, heals the sick, and comforts the weary? To this question, the answer is a quick and definite *Yes!*

Let any interested person agree to drop his present "belief" or "faith" and retire each day to some quiet place for contemplation or meditation, and surrender himself in the sense of: Let faith be established in me. Let faith be revealed within me. May that which is God fill me with His faith—not mine. In quietness and confidence I await the unfoldment of the true faith—that which God will impart to me in some understandable way. This, of course, will not be a formula: you will take this theme into consciousness and let it formulate itself in your own words and thoughts. Above all, remember that it is in quietness and confidence that you await the establishment of God's faith and His vision within you. Faith is not something generated in us toward God, but a quality and an activity of God, imparted by Him to us. Await His grace with confident assurance.

Not many days or weeks of inner contemplation will be required before you literally "feel" faith being revealed and established within you. Never again will you ignorantly worship or blindly believe —*now you will know and understand faith,* and you will witness the "signs following."

Along with faith will come love—a love of God which passeth all understanding. Heretofore we have only given lip service to love of God, but with the first warm glow of faith comes a love which embraces God and all His creation. Until the faith of God is established in one, faith is weak and faltering—and love of God is but a phrase. Touched by His faith, Love enters the Soul with its healing ministry—and the sick are healed, the hungry fed, the naked clothed, and His kingdom is established within *you.*

You cannot have faith in God—but God can, and will, establish His faith in you. Approach God, in the inner stillness, with confidence that it is His will that we know His faith, His will, His love— and be receptive to Him. Then will come the crowning glory—a life lived by faith—His faith in you.

THE INFINITE WAY LESSON FOR CHILDREN

Obedience

Aloha, Young Friends! Do you recall our last lesson in which was emphasized the fact that it was your responsibility to be the emissaries to carry God's love and peace wherever you may go? I wonder if you memorized the Master's loving words, "Peace I leave with you, my peace I give unto you,"—and if you are remembering them as you go about your daily activities? If so, you are obeying the two greatest Commandments—to love the Lord with all thy heart, and with all thy soul, and with all thy mind; and thy neighbor as thyself—and you are being a good child of God. By the way, these same two Commandments appear in the Old Testament as well as in the New Testament. If you will take your Bible and turn to the 20th chapter of Exodus, you will find the first and greatest Commandment stated in somewhat different words but having the same meaning: "Thou shalt have no other gods before me." And in the 19th chapter of Leviticus, you will find "Thou shalt love thy neighbor as thyself." Why not look up these passages right now?

Just as these commandments are teachings of the Hebrew faith as well as the Christian, they are also the teachings of faiths the world over. Someday, perhaps we will take a little journey into some of the other bibles of the world where we will find that love for God and love for our neighbor is a teaching older than time, and one that has been embraced by all other religions and all other peoples. When we understand this, it makes it much simpler and easier to love our neighbor. We must realize, of course, that the term "neighbor" does not necessarily mean the people who live next door or down the street. It is more far-reaching than that. Our neighbor is every person or animal or thing that lives in the world, regardless of race, color, religion, type, kind, or location. Our neighbor lives in Asia, Africa, China, Europe, North America, South America. Our pets are our neighbors, and even the plants growing in our gardens.

Let us now take another step on the path of The Infinite Way. If you looked up the Ten Commandments (and surely you have read them!) you found one which says: "Honor thy father and thy mother; that thy days may be long upon the land which the Lord thy God giveth thee." Now, we must be perfectly honest and straightforward with each other, and realize that if we are to receive God's blessings we must obey His Commandments. There is no other way. So ask yourselves this question: Am I honoring my father and mother? Think this over very carefully, and meanwhile let me show you how to obey this Commandment in a very simple and beautiful way.

Have you ever stopped to consider that when you apply yourself and receive good marks, both in school work and in conduct, you are honoring your father and mother? You are being a credit to them, by showing forth the results of their care and discipline and love. Whatever commendation you receive, they receive by reflection. Every time you receive an honor in the way of a medal, an appointment, or even an "A" on your report card, remember that you did not do it all by yourself: your parents helped you to that distinction, and without their help you never would have achieved it—no more than you would have achieved it without the help of God!

In everything you do, you have three partners—God, your father, and your mother. Without their help you cannot accomplish very much, so always be sure to acknowledge the part they play in your experience. The world, however, will acknowledge their help, even if you forget, because the world knows that you would have no achievements for which to be honored were it not for the love and blessings of God and the love and care and protection of your parents. If you become known as an obedient and thoughtful son or daughter, or if you are a good or outstanding student, do not make the mistake of thinking that you receive all the glory. God is glorified in your achievements, and your parents share that glory. All the good that the world thinks about you reflects a credit upon your parents, and so if you do nothing more than achieve good marks or a reputation for being kind and good and generous, you are honoring your father and mother, and thereby also honoring God.

Now, let us look at this from another standpoint. Whenever you get into trouble, or do an unkind thing, or get poor grades, you are, in a measure, discrediting your father and mother. Whenever you are inclined to neglect your studies or chores and let things slide by, or whenever you are thoughtless, disrespectful, or selfish, an unfavorable reflection is cast upon their care and discipline. So when these temptations come to you, do not think you are the only one to be considered—think of whether or not you would be honoring, or dishonoring, your father and mother.

There is a spiritual reason behind the Commandment to honor your father and mother. God is your real Father-Mother, and your earthly parents are His direct deputies to whom are entrusted the responsibility and privilege of representing and establishing God's care, protection, discipline, and love in your lives. Therefore, in honoring your parents you are honoring God. You can readily see that your obedience toward your parents, your attitude and conduct toward all people, and your application to studies and work, all go hand in hand: because when you remember the Commandment to honor your father and mother it will naturally follow that you will remember to love God, and that, in turn, will lead you to remember to love your neighbor as yourself.

These three Commandments always go together— side by side. They entail rather a grave responsibility for young people, but it is a responsibility that you must assume. You do not love and honor God except as you love and honor your parents. You do not love God except in the love you exhibit to your neighbors, whether they be everyday friends or people whom you will never meet. Therefore, in honoring your father and mother and in loving your neighbor, you are automatically loving God. As you ponder and meditate upon this idea you will realize that love, peace, obedience, and honor all blend together into one beautiful theme to make your lives, and the lives of others, joyous, happy, and harmonious.

Anandashram: a Spiritual Haven
When Swami Ramdas was on his world tour last

year, I was in India when his party arrived in Honolulu, and it was the privilege of one of our students to be hostess to the spiritual pilgrims. It was inevitable that on another trip I would find myself a guest at Anandashram.

Those who know Swami Ramdas, or who are familiar with his writings, already realize that here is a God-conscious individual. The very first impression on entering the gate at Anandashram is that here is the natural fruitage of God realization. Enormous grounds set in the rolling hills of South India, many modern houses, bungalows, and administration and temple buildings surprise the visitor still thinking in terms of material India.

Here the first lesson of Swami Ramdas' ministry is learned—"To the pure, all things are pure." So to those rich in spiritual awareness, the whole world is revealed in beauty, grace, and abundance. It is wise to ponder this lesson—otherwise, the vision of spiritual consciousness is lost. Only out of the depth of spiritual richness can such abundance and beauty flow!

The practical side of spiritual understanding is likewise revealed in the comfort of the quarters provided for guests, the care of the sick, the ample provisions for the temporarily needy, the plates set for hundreds of visitors. When the spiritual attainment of one man can express itself in the harmony, peace, and graciousness so amply visible here, it behooves all of us to strive for more of this realized Grace. Visitors, guests, associates, and workers unite in a great love for Swami Ramdas and Mother Krishnabai—and their love is deeply felt as it embraces first the kingdom of God and then this universe within it.

Probably, because our Infinite Way reveals that the attainment of the realization of God-presence results in the harmony of body and all daily experience, my greatest reaction here is that the God realization of Swami Ramdas exemplifies exactly this in the practical unfoldment of Anandashram. The peace and joy of his soul are evident in the harmony of all the relationships met here; the richness of his spiritual consciousness is evident in the abundance that greets one in every corner of this estate; the poise and orderliness of the Swami's life are expressed in the harmonious functioning of this large establishment.

The Swami has attained freedom within—and he gives freedom to all. Here is a complete absence of rules and regulations, and yet a perfect rhythm brings us all to meditation in the Ashram at five o'clock in the morning, to devotional readings during the day, and meditations at night.

The physical setting of Anandashram is ideally suited to periods of prayer, meditation and devotion —and always there is the awareness that even the grounds and buildings are maintained in a constant spiritual communion. Here, too, is exemplified "Except the Lord build the house, they labor in vain that build it" since here is visible proof that the Lord has builded this Temple Anandashram, and Swami Ramdas has dedicated it to His Holy Name.

Across the Desk

Travelling the world reveals clearly that there is

no hope of ultimate "peace on earth" through any of the recognized means.

Once upon a time, peace was maintained by bows and arrows, lances and swords. Later, those who had guns subdued those who did not have them—and so a better way was found to have "peace". As the power of weapons increased, peace was merely a matter of bigger and better arms. But lo! it is now impossible for one nation, or group of nations, to go to war: the might of weapons is such that whole continents can be destroyed; but the weapons may backfire and destroy the destroyers, so this means of maintaining peace is obsolete. Another era saw peace maintained by treaties. But treaties first became "scraps of paper"—then later merely temporary matters of convenience to be regarded or disregarded at will. Even the United Nations is founded on the assumption that it is only necessary to honor a commitment if it suits the immediate convenience—otherwise, veto it! So I repeat: none of the heretofore recognized means of attaining or maintaining peace will avail in this age.

Travelling also reveals that it is being thought and recognized, more and more, that there must now rise a spiritual teacher, or teaching, to lead the way to peace. But I say to you that no spiritual teacher or teaching is necessary. It will be sufficient to recognize and acknowledge the power of Spirit in the teachers and teachings now available in every country on the globe. To understand that the same Spirit animates the great teachers, teachings, and followers the world over; to realize the need for all these to unite in prayer, even while maintaining the individuality of every group; to "see" that the one Power is Love—here we have the new formula for peace.

To rightly understand The Infinite Way is to behold the measure of Christ, Truth, Love, revealed in all teachings. This better enables us "to love our neighbor as ourselves." The Infinite Way recognizes that the one holy Spirit, the one pure Soul, animates and governs every spiritual teacher and teaching. It acknowledges that this mighty God-power, acting as the consciousness of spiritually minded individuals all around the globe, unites us in eternal peace. The Infinite Way visualizes the day when it shall be universally proclaimed: "There is but one God, one Son, the Spirit of God in man; one holy family united in His Being."

To God, "neither circumcision, nor uncircumcision availeth." To God, it is of no account in what form men worship; nor how clothed. God's peace descends upon all equally who unite in recognition of one Power, one Presence, one supreme Being. God's peace will be revealed on earth when men unite in agreement to accept one Love as the universal government in the hearts of every religion and nation. Each may follow his own religious rites, ritual, ceremonies; each may follow his own flag and form of government; but must remain united in one supreme God, as the Creator and Sustainer of all men equally, everywhere.

As The Infinite Way has realized this Oneness operating as individual consciousness, many ministers, rabbis, swamis, and mystics of no title, have likewise opened their hearts and minds to us. The universal nature of Love prompts these friends to love us and our work, and we have found peace in each other. No doubt many of you, sooner or later, will be travelling in far parts of the globe, and you will be glad to find such friends ready to greet you.

Conquerors have travelled from land to land and across many seas to overcome, subdue, capture, and exploit other peoples and nations. Churches have sent their missionaries to win whole races to their forms and doctrines and beliefs. And now, The Infinite Way travels the entire universe to unite the family of men in the love of, and under the government of, one supreme Being. You may worship It as God, Christ, Emmanuel, Tao, Brahm, Buddha—but recognize It as the one Infinite Invisible appearing as the consciousness of individual man, whoever he may be, or where, or when. God is equally the God of the past, present, and future, appearing *now* as the mind and law of those who accept one universal Life and Love as the animating principle of all.

THE NEW INFINITE WAY

by

Henry Thomas Hamblin

As promised, I am giving some more particulars of Joel Goldsmith's additional chapter to the new edition of *The Infinite Way*, entitled "Wisdoms of The Infinite Way."

Some readers may experience some difficulty in following him, but this need not be the case if they remember that Joel Goldsmith is speaking from the point of view of the Absolute: that is, God as infinite perfection, wholeness, and completeness. Nothing has *to be*, but everything *is*. In addition to a number of very deep and cryptic sayings, Joel gives some hints on meditation. He says, "There are two stages of meditation, serving two distinct purposes. The normal person lives a life entirely in the external—working, enjoying, and playing, physically and mentally. His laws are physical, mental, and legal. His instruction is from persons or books. At some period he learns that 'the Kingdom of God is within you' and an interest in this Kingdom is awakened. Probably now he finds himself pondering the significance of the statement, 'the Kingdom of God is within you.' This is his first meditation.

"As this meditation becomes a daily experience, two, three, and four times a day, an expansion of consciousness takes place, and as more and more of this infinite storehouse of wisdom, law, and power is revealed, he learns to depend less and less on outer forms of force, power, law, or knowledge.

"Finally there dawns in consciousness the tremendous experience of understanding that since the Kingdom of God is within me, and the King, God, is ever within His Realm—within me—that direct impartation of wisdom, direction, law, and power *can* come to me, and he is then ready to remember the boy, Samuel—'Speak, Lord: for thy servant heareth'."

Many people expect to go straight ahead without meeting with any disasters in the spiritual life. Joel speaks of this in a very helpful way. He says, "When the house of cards (of the spiritual student) crumbles, he is near to the house 'not made with hands'. Spiritual student—Rejoice! as the outer building tumbles down—for the Inner Temple is to be revealed. It is impossible to realize God as long as one has a 'purpose' or 'object' in mind— other than realizing God." Here is another wise word: "The crucifixion of the self is accomplished when there is nothing left for which we wish to pray."

Some people imagine that those who are in the Spiritual Path should never meet with difficulties and discordant experiences. Joel, however, points out that we have to meet with these things and that we cannot escape them. He says, "To those unfolding on the Spiritual Path come the discordant experiences of human life, until the transition from 'this world' has been completely accomplished. The *desire* is to escape these inharmonies of mind, body, or economic affairs. The tendency is to avoid or escape them— but this cannot be done, since the discords result solely from the battle between Spirit and 'the flesh'— that is, spiritual consciousness and material sense."

It is not possible for me to say any more this month, but what I have said will surely arouse the interest of true seekers after God.

Reprinted from *Science of Thought Review*, April, 1956.   Chichester, Sussex, England

CHAPTER SEVEN

TRANSITION FROM LAW TO GRACE

Now faith is the substance of things hoped for, the evidence of things not seen. . . . Through faith we understand that the worlds were framed by the word of God, so that things which are seen were not made of things which do appear.

Hebrews 11:1, 3

EVEN as Abraham, the father of the Hebrew race, journeyed long distances in time and space, not knowing whereto or why, so must we travel long distances in consciousness to arrive at a destined place where is found heaven—spiritual harmony, spiritual freedom, spiritual grace. We, as Infinite Way students, are pilgrims on that journey. All of us are seeking a life by grace, and in order to make any progress on this spiritual journey, we must understand the importance of faith in the unknown.

As human beings, from the moment of conception until the moment of death, we are under the law of Moses, which is a karmic law. We are under the laws of nature, of weather, climate, food, race, religion, creed, dogma. We are under the law of revenge —an eye for an eye, a tooth for a tooth. These Mosaic and karmic laws are made up of both good and evil. We do not choose to come under the law —we are under the law simply by virtue of being born, and we remain under the law until we, individually, remove ourselves from it. There are no ministers, priests, or rabbis who can set aside the law of the Ten Commandments, the karmic law, or the laws of human nature. It is something each one must do for himself by an act of consciousness. It is something you must do as specifically as you must resist the various temptations that crowd your particular individual life—by an act of conscious will. If you are tempted to envy that which others possess, it is you who, by an act of consciousness, must determine to be satisfied with that which is received from God and to covet nothing that belongs to another. If the temptations were to come to steal, to lie, to commit adultery, you would have to reject these temptations, individually, specifically, and consciously.

When the Master was tempted to demonstrate supply by turning stones into bread, his understanding was, No!—that which is to come to me must come of God, not of my personal powers. Three times in that wilderness experience Jesus rejected temptation by a conscious act of mind, a conscious act of will, by a conscious act of Soul. As his ministry progressed, every time he was tempted to behold sin, disease, lack, or death, he specifically rejected them by refusing to accept such appearances. "Get thee behind me, Satan. . . . Arise, and take up thy bed. . . . Neither hath this man sinned, nor his parents. . . . Neither do I condemn thee." Because the Master was enabled to reject such temptations, many people believe that we will be spared these experiences, but it is not true. Each one of us is subject to temptations from the time he is born until he dies; subject to the laws of good and evil; subject to laws which benefit and bless one day, and turn and rend the next.

In speaking to the Galatians, Paul said: "Be not deceived; God is not mocked: for whatsoever a man soweth, that shall he also reap. For he that soweth to his flesh shall of the flesh reap corruption: but he that soweth to the Spirit shall of the Spirit reap life everlasting." This is not a Christian law, but an old Hebrew or Mosaic law, whereby we are given the choice of deciding for ourselves whether we shall sow to the flesh or to the Spirit.

All human experience is based on material conditions and things. Therefore, to sow to the flesh means to have faith in matter. If you place your faith in the creature, that is, in persons, dollars, climate, materia medica, et cetera, you must reap the fruits of such material beliefs. If, in any way, you place your faith in material substance, you must take the evil along with the good, the old as well as the young, the sick as well as the healthy, the poor as well as the rich. For instance, if you place your faith for life in the body, eventually you will lose your life. Life is not in the body, life is in God; and if you place faith in the organs and functions of the body, that very faith will trap and ensnare you.

On the other hand, to sow to the Spirit is to understand that there is an invisible Something or Substance—an invisible Presence which is your life, and in which you place your entire faith. This Something can in no way be discerned by the human senses.

It cannot be seen, heard, touched, tasted, or smelled —neither can It be reasoned with, nor will It discuss Itself. This invisible Something speaks the Word, and either you can obey and reap life everlasting, or you can reject It and pay the penalty of the flesh. The choice is yours. If your faith is in the Spirit, you will obey without question.

In the interpretation of Nebuchadnezzar's dream, the prophet Daniel revealed that the great image, made of gold, silver, brass, iron, and clay, which represented the kingdoms of earth (materiality), was destroyed by a "stone . . . cut out of the mountain without hands." He further revealed that "the God of heaven [shall] set up a kingdom which shall never be destroyed . . . but it shall break in pieces and consume all these kingdoms, and it shall stand for ever." What is this stone but faith in and understanding of the Invisible? If one were to use one's hands to cut the stone, one would be resorting to material power; but when the stone is cut without hands, one is relying upon that which is unknown to human sense —spiritual power. This spiritual power will destroy the temporal kingdoms.

As human beings, what are we doing? Are we destroying the kingdoms of materiality, or placing our faith in them? To a great extent the answer is clear: our faith is in persons and things—in money, food, climate, drugs, in business and pleasures. All of these things have failed us. Even our governments and the men we have chosen to lead us with wisdom and justice have led us into one war after another. Ultimately, everything that may be called the creature fails us. Paul tells us that those who worship and serve the creature more than the Creator, change the truth of God into a lie. The Creator is invisible. Reality, "the substance of things hoped for," is invisible, even intangible to human sense, and yet that is where we must place our faith.

If you have come to the point of decision where you are willing, honestly and earnestly, to review the past twenty, thirty, or forty years of your life, ask yourself if any of the kingdoms of "this world" have ever come up to your expectations or have ever really stood up for you. When you come to the realization that they always have, and always will fail and disappoint, you are led to make that tremendous, yet courageous, step into the unknown. It is then that you make the supreme act of faith in which, henceforth, your resolve is to live by virtue of the Invisible; by virtue of that upon which you cannot lay your hands, and which even eludes thought! It is by this undeviating decision to live by faith that you will find yourself, actually and literally, living by grace.

To the world at large it is impossible to speak of living by grace, but to those with some metaphysical background, it is more understandable. Most metaphysicians have witnessed healings that cannot be accounted for by material means, and there is a greater inclination to accept the fact that there is active in human consciousness an invisible Presence or Power which can, and will, take over if given the opportunity. From the very moment that you are willing to "come out from among them and be separate" by accepting the government of divine grace, the law no longer operates in your experience.

Once you make the transition from the law to grace, you are set free; your sins are forgiven; and you are no longer under the law of punishment.

To some degree we are all sinners, and it is inevitable and automatic that we pay the penalty for violating the law. If you accept the good of the law, you must also be willing to accept the evil: in other words, if you accept the benefit of the violation, you must expect to pay the penalty for the violation. But from the moment you determine that your life shall be lived by grace, all past offences are erased and forgiven. Although the full evidence of grace may not be apparent immediately, as the weeks and months pass you will find the penalties for those past physical, mental, or moral offences gradually dropping away. Though your sins were scarlet, they will be white as snow. The woman taken in adultery was forgiven and instantly released from the penalty of her sins! The thief on the cross was taken into paradise that very night!

The Master was well aware of the possibility of returning to the old state of human consciousness when he said: "Behold, thou art made whole: sin no more, lest a worse thing come unto thee." Once we are forgiven it is imperative that we heed that admonition, and in order to avoid going back, we must definitely begin to accept faith as the infinite, invisible Presence and Power governing us and appearing outwardly as the substance of those things hoped for—the evidence of things not seen.

While we look not at the things which are seen, but at the things which are not seen: for the things which are seen are temporal; but the things which are not seen are eternal.

II Corinthians 4:18

Receptivity

Certainly the decision to live by grace is desirable, but it is not an easy decision to make, nor is it a simple one to follow. By way of illustration, whereby we may understand how to go about it, I will use myself as an example. After seating myself comfortably in a quiet place, and after stilling my thoughts by shutting out the world as much as possible, I will say within myself: "I and my Father are one. All that the Father hath is mine. The kingdom of God, the allness of God, the completeness and perfection of God, is within me. As a child of God, I am an heir to all the heavenly riches, joint-heir with all other children of God. The place whereon I stand is holy ground, so that right here I, Joel, have the wholeness of the kingdom of God flowing to me and through me. The fullness of the Godhead is expressing Itself as the health, harmony, supply, intelligence, wisdom, wholeness, completeness, purity, and infinity of my being! All that the Father hath is mine!"

From the moment that decision is made there is an important fact to remember: I dare not look to the world with a feeling that anyone owes me something, that anyone can give me something, or that I deserve something. Henceforth I must live in that purity. I must know this regarding health: I dare not say, "This little tablet will relieve my headache." I must know this regarding supply: I dare not wonder, "Where can I borrow this necessary sum of money?" I must know this about completeness: I dare not indulge my loneliness and hope that someone will befriend or love me. No! I have made my declaration of faith in the Invisible, and I will stand by it! ". . . he that seeth me seeth him that sent me"—for we are one.

Thus it is with all of us. For instance, a married woman may receive her income and support from her husband, but she must not believe he owes it to her, or that the marriage bond entitles her to it. The kingdom of God is within her, and her supply is of God, although God is expressing it through her husband. No one, under grace, should think that anyone in the world owes him anything—not even a debt of gratitude or a debt of love. Nothing! "I and my Father are one. . . . All things that the Father hath are mine."

Is it not strange, as we read the words of the Master, how often a completely new meaning is unfolded in consciousness? Sometimes it seems as if we were reading them for the first time. "Before Abraham was, I am. . . . Lo, I am with you alway, even unto the end of the world." As we comprehend these familiar words in the light of new understanding, we find another reason why we must not put our faith in matter, in the creature, or in anything that is formed: in order to live by grace our faith must be transferred to the Invisible, to the Unknown. It takes courage to stand on that. It takes courage to go without a medicine on which one has relied. It takes courage to move thousands of miles without knowing any reason for it. It takes courage to look away from all one's human sources of good and inwardly hold to the fact that I have a divine Source of good—the Spirit of God that is within me. This transition from reliance on human means to complete reliance on faith in the Invisible is an act of conscious realization, and one which every individual must make for himself—otherwise he remains under the law with only the arm of flesh for provision and protection.

In the last World War we had nothing but block-busters to worry about, but now we have atomic bombs and hydrogen bombs. Who can build shelters against such weapons? Is there no hope for man? No!—there is no hope for man who is depending on more and better matter to support, maintain, and save his life; no hope for man who is looking to covenants for protection, to governments for support. Where or when is it ever going to end if we are always to continue living under the law of law?

Unfortunately, those of us who live in the United States have witnessed a whole new series of governments and laws and regulations by means of which they have tried to convince us that man's glorious purpose on earth is to feed and maintain the State—even if it takes 90 percent of what he earns to do it. For 150 years our country grew from a handful of sturdy and clear-sighted pioneers under the ideology and teaching that the State was for the citizen, and that the government was maintained for the benefit of the citizen. But now they would have us believe that that was all a mistake, and that it is the citizen's duty to give everything to the State in order to feed and maintain an autocracy!

This is far removed from God's grace. This is getting away from the fact that there is an invisible Presence and Power which is capable of supporting every individual on the face of the globe and which, through the individual, can maintain whatever of a State is necessary.

All our lives our faith has been in that which is visible, in that which can be known and understood by the senses. But that was because we did not understand what the Master meant when he said: "Man shall not live by bread alone, but by every word that proceedeth out of the mouth of God." And yet that one statement is our shibboleth—our password into heaven. That statement will take any one of us out from under the law into a life by grace, because whenever you are tempted to turn stones into bread to fulfill your needs and desires, or to work a miracle in order to be free of sin, disease, or death, the password, "Man shall not live by bread alone, but by every word that proceedeth out of the mouth of God," will be your blessing and benediction.

"The heathen raged, the kingdoms were moved: he uttered his voice, the earth melted." This is the Psalmist's way of telling us that every time God utters His voice in you, or in me, some earthly discord or error fades away. There is only one thing necessary for our salvation, and it is nothing that can be found in any creature or in any thing that is formed. This one necessity is the ability to hear the still, small voice of God—and, hearing It, to obey!

This brings us to the crux of the entire situation.

Have we the ability to hear the still, small Voice? To most people the answer is No! Having lived for generations in a sense of separation from God, giving ear to, and being swayed by, the thoughts and opinions and theories of man whose breath is in his nostrils, we have not trained ourselves to listen and to hear the Voice that is always whispering and uttering Itself within us. We have not learned to turn within, but now we have come to this period of our lives where we must begin. Experience has shown that for those who have not learned to hear the Voice and to be guided by It, there is a way to achieve it. The way is through meditation.

Except for the few who have been trained to think and live spiritually, and who have learned to abide somewhat within themselves, meditation is not easy. From any standpoint it is a difficult thing to learn. My own experience was probably much more difficult than it will be for you because my background was such that I never had been taught introspection, nor was I what would be called a thinker or reasoner. Always having been the intuitive type, whenever I needed any knowledge, it just came to the end of my fingers or to the tip of my tongue. And so, when I came to meditation it was eight months before I received the very first "click"— eight long months of turning within: at first, six, eight, ten times a day; later, twelve and twenty times.

I doubt if it will prove that difficult or long for you, but even if it should it is well worth while. A few months are nothing to give up compared to the joy that is yours once you attain the ability to still the human mind and hear the voice of God. Verily, from that day you can say, with Paul: "I live; yet not I, but Christ liveth in me: and the life which I now live in the flesh I live by the faith of the Son of God . . ."—and demonstrate it! From that time on, Christ tells you what to do and when to do it. Christ guides, leads, protects—not the Man of Galilee, but Christ, the Spirit of God within you! That Spirit is there, right now, even if you have not yet learned to attune yourself and make contact with it. It is as omnipresent as are the thousand melodies waiting this moment to be heard, as omnipresent as are the thousand books waiting to be written—all are being broadcast within you at this very moment, and they are just awaiting your ability to tune in and hear that still, small Voice.

Man need not live by bread alone. Man need not live by law; therefore he need not consider the law. His sins will be forgiven so that he does not have to pay the penalty; earthly errors will melt away— but in order to live by the Word that proceedeth out of the mouth of God, he must develop the ability to hear the Voice that is uttered within himself.

The beginning of that process is not difficult. Begin by recalling as many passages of truth as you can remember, more especially the wisdom of the Master, bringing these words to conscious remembrance whenever the temptation arises to say you need this, you desire that, or that you are owed or deserve something. Whenever tempted with such thoughts, reject them with the realization: "No! I am not living by bread alone. I am living by the Word of God. I am living by virtue of the *I* at the center of my being. That *I* will never leave me, nor forsake me. I am living on the promise that *I* will provide—the *I* that was with me before Abraham; the *I* that will be with me until the end of the world. The flames will not burn, the waters will not drown, the valley of the shadow of death will hold no terrors, for *I* am with me."

You will soon find that this is not a work for a lazy man for you must make a diligent and unceasing effort to learn and apply these passages, thereby making them a living part of your consciousness. There is no God sitting on a heavenly cloud waiting to reward you when you say the right words or think the right thoughts. There *is* a God, but He is at the center of your own being—the Word is in the midst of you and, as Browning writes, you must open out a way for the imprisoned splendor to escape. All the great words of spiritual wisdom are within you; they were within you before Abraham was, but you must utter them with your mouth, think them with your mind, recall them with your memory; and every time there is a tendency to return to the thoughts and things and ways of the world, you must bring them to conscious remembrance so that truly you can begin to say, "No longer do I live by bread alone—each day I live more and more in the consciousness of the Word that proceedeth out of the mouth of God."

THE INFINITE WAY LESSON FOR CHILDREN

The Universality of Truth

Uppermost in our hearts is the desire to be good

children of God. It is the purpose of The Infinite Way to teach us that God is our Father-Mother, and that in order to be good children of God we must obey his commandments. The two most important commandments are that we love God, and that we love our neighbor as ourselves. And so, if we are to love God, we must love every other child of God, regardless of race, religion, color, or creed.

As this is our last lesson for the time being, we shall review the various points which have been brought forth in our previous lessons to see how they all fit together, and we shall find that it is in observance of these various points that we are obeying the laws of God. As I promised, we will take a little journey into some of the scriptures of other peoples, whereby we will find that many of their teachings present the same truths as those presented in our own Bible.

First we shall go to China: "Be always studious to be in harmony with the laws of God, and you will obtain much happiness." Did we not learn the very same thing—that if we are to receive God's blessings we must obey His commandments? Obedience and happiness always go together, do they not?

Previously we learned that whatever we hold in consciousness will be shouted from the housetops—in other words, whatever we think or say or do in that little secret place within our hearts will be sensed and known to all the world. In the Hindu-Buddhist Scriptures of India, we find this same thought presented as follows: "If a man speaks or acts with a pure thought, happiness follows him like a shadow that never leaves him." Also: "Be kind to all creatures that have life. Do not speak harshly to anyone." We shall stop for a moment in Persia: "He is happy who makes others happy." Now we go to Turkey where, in the Mohammedan Scriptures, we read: "There is not an animal on earth, nor a flying creature flying on two wings, but they are peoples like unto you." Is this not what Jesus said about loving our neighbor as ourself?

We shall linger a little longer in Turkey because as we read further we come across a very beautiful passage: "Your God is one God. He it is who created you and all of us in the earth. He taketh care of all things. Not a leaf falleth but He knoweth it; nor a grain amid the darkness of the earth. Do thou remember the Lord within thyself, humbly and withal; behold thy breath at morn and evening, and in the night time also; hymn Him His praise and at the setting of the stars." In our own Bible, this same truth is given in these words: "Hear, O Israel: the Lord our God is one Lord." As we search further we are always finding similar truths. For instance: "Are not two sparrows sold for a farthing? and one of them shall not fall on the ground without your Father. But the very hairs of your head are all numbered. Fear ye not therefore, ye are of more value than many sparrows. . . . Therefore rejoice, ye heavens, and ye that dwell in them. . . . Let us be glad and rejoice, and give honor to him."

If you will turn to the fifth chapter of Matthew, you will find the Sermon on the Mount wherein Jesus set forth a model way of life. Later on it would be well if you were to read and study this entire chapter, but just now we shall touch on only a few verses: "Blessed are the meek: for they shall inherit the earth. . . . Blessed are the merciful: for they shall obtain mercy. Blessed are the peacemakers: for they shall be called the children of God. . . . Come, ye blessed of my Father, inherit the kingdom prepared for you from the foundation of the world."

All of these scriptural passages bring out the universality of love, obedience, and peace. When we took up the subject of love, we learned that God is love, and that our purpose on earth is to express love in our lives and to be a channel through which love finds its way to others. If you studied these lessons well, you will remember that love is just another name for peace. When Jesus taught, "Blessed are the peacemakers: for they shall be called the children of God," he was saying that you must assume the responsibility of carrying love and peace into all your everyday endeavors, identifying yourself with the idea that you are a peacemaker bestowing the love and peace of God upon all whom you encounter. If, during the course of the day, you chance to meet someone who is ill or unhappy, speak these words silently within yourself: "My peace I give unto you." You will almost be able to see the peace of mind and soul, health and happiness steal over the faces of those so lovingly blessed. If the peace of God rules in your hearts, truly you can say, "In him we live, and move, and have our being," and be able to convey this peace to others.

Hawaii is called the Crossroads of the Pacific because the population is composed of native Hawaiians, Japanese, Chinese, Filipinos, Samoans,

Fijians, as well as natives of North and South America, England, Europe, and all the other countries of the world. All these races, cultures, religions, and creeds cross and intermingle constantly, and yet these people are able to live and work and play together harmoniously, joyously, and peacefully. Instead of arguing or discussing differences, always they are able to find some common meeting ground of truth upon which they can unite. In observing these people, I have learned that there are three things we must do, and for which we are responsible, that will hasten the day when there will be true peace on earth and good will toward all men: First, obedience to the commandment to love God; second, to love our neighbor as ourself. The third is the lesson we learned from the last *Letter*—honor your father and mother by being deserving of honors; because, if you will recall, all the honor and respect and love that the world pays you is, in reality, honoring your father and mother—and thereby honoring God. "Let your light so shine before men, that they may see your good works, and glorify your Father which is in heaven."

Love, obedience, honor, and peace—these are the messengers heralding the kingdom of God on earth. In farewell, once more I say, Aloha. May the love of God shine upon you and keep you in perfect peace.

The True Basis of Religion

The following is the text of my first talk given in the presence of Swami Ramdas to the devotees assembled at the Ashram Bhajan Hall, on December 8th, 1955, while I was a visitor at the Ashram.

In the beginning, the true religious teaching, originating with Krishna and Buddha, made its way from the East to the West, and wherever it travelled and whatever its source through human consciousness, it touched men to the realization of their own spiritual being. The teaching went from India to China, to Japan and then into Egypt, gradually making its way to the Hebrew Holy Land. Always it was the same truth—the teaching of one God, one Supreme Being—and that this great spiritual power is inherent in all men.

The time came when this truth touched a Hebrew rabbi who saw that in the organized church the pure teaching of man's individual spiritual powers was being lost. And so, once again, as Jesus preached by the seaside and on the hills, he taught a truth so profound that in every ensuing age it is repeated: the spiritual kingdom is not of this world—*"The kingdom of God is within you!"*

I do not come from the West to the East to be a teacher: instead, I come to visit the teachers of the East because the teaching of the East is now that of the West. Now we are all one in a spiritual brotherhood of such far-reaching power that even before we meet, the true teachers of both the East and the West are known to each other. This is felt inwardly. The true teacher is drawn to the true teacher, just as the true student is drawn to the true teacher. And so, in visiting you, this is my means of acknowledging the spiritual teacher and teaching that is embodied in our Swami Ramdas. This is the acknowledgment and realization that the Light of the World, which is spiritual wisdom, is here embodied. Like all seekers, I also come to seek and receive more of that Light.

The true teachings of spiritual wisdom are to be found in the scriptures of all peoples: it is in the *Bhagavad Gita*, in the *Upanishads*, in the *Vedas*, in the Bible. Knowledge can be found in all of these inspired writings, but there is one essential point that too often is overlooked: the light of spiritual wisdom can be found only in those men and women of illumined consciousness. Here is the central point of all religion.

Most of the world is satisfied and content to seek its religion in books, to read these words of wisdom and to think that that is all the wisdom to be attained, and to believe that thereby they are reaching the kingdom of heaven. Nothing could be farther from the truth. No one can ever reach the kingdom of heaven through knowledge obtained from books. The kingdom of heaven is attained only through spiritual revelation and spiritual realization! When this realization comes to an individual, that individual is a teacher, and he becomes the Light of the World, first in his own immediate circles and later to greater and ever-widening circles. It is through contact with such an illumined consciousness that we, individually, are enabled to attain the light of realization. Therefore, each one must find his teacher and receive the light through him.

Always this fact has been known in the East, more especially in India. In Japan, in some forms of Buddhism, such as Zen Buddhism, the guru system also is known. A spiritual master is enabled to lift the student to the light—not always to the same height as that attained by the teacher, however, because it is imperative that each one who receives a glimpse of realization must, after that, attempt to lift himself further and higher into his own God consciousness. The Western world has not always known this. Until recently we have read the Bible and other sacred literature, affiliated ourselves with churches, listened to sermons, and prayed. Only now is it beginning to be known in the West that only one who is spiritually illumined can lift others who desire that same illumination.

This is the true basis of religion: each individual must be illumined to the point of receiving God consciousness, of attaining God realization. It is true, of course, that the knowledge to be found in books is helpful and of great benefit, but the ultimate achievement comes as we bring ourselves into the association of saints, and into contact with those men and women who have achieved God realization. They, through the grace of God, are enabled to raise and lift us in consciousness in the degree that we are fitted for it.

Now that we are aware of this basic fact, we must go one step further and understand that in seeking the spiritual light of a teacher we must not be seeking merely to improve our health, our wealth, our homes, or business. We must seek the light for one reason: that the old self may die and that we may be reborn of the Spirit. Many people seek God hoping that He will make their human lives happier, healthier, and wealthier. If we approach God from that standpoint, He will still be a God afar off, able to help us in one way perhaps, but willing to deny us in another. The ancient teaching of the East reveals that this is not true. Rather, it reveals that the old human self must die, and that the new Godself be born in us so that we are no longer desirous of more and more of the so-called good things of human existence; that we must rise ever higher into the desire for God's gifts of spiritual wisdom, spiritual light, spiritual guidance, spiritual health, spiritual supply—all the things that are ours by grace once we die to our personal selfhood.

Self-consciousness imposes upon us the human law of self-preservation in which we seek to save and enrich ourselves even at the expense of others. Under this law one nation attempts to live even if another nation must die; one nation attains freedom even if another is enslaved. But true Self-consciousness, true Self-realization, true God consciousness is a release from all human aspirations and propensities, and brings with it the capacity to share God's spiritual freedom and joy with all mankind. As an individual receives the first gleam of this pure spiritual light, this sense of self-preservation and self-benefit is lost, and there arises in him the desire to receive more and more of the light of spiritual illumination and power, more of God's grace.

Eventually, there comes the day when he is born into the second stage of enlightenment, whereby he loses even the desire to seek more spiritual light. In that day the man is dead to all sense of self and there is revealed "the new man, which after God is created in righteousness and true holiness." Then it is that the spiritual light is free to flow to all who will earnestly and humbly touch the consciousness of that light. Although the light may still appear as a teacher such as Swami Ramdas or some other illumined individual, in reality it is not. In our ignorance of the spiritual kingdom we see the man, but when viewed from the heights of divine Consciousness only the light remains.

In our Western world it is said that we cannot follow the spiritual path because it is not practicable and operative in our everyday affairs. However, it has been proven time and time again that the spiritual life is by far the most feasible life, and the reason is this: when the spiritual light touches an individual's consciousness, he becomes more proficient and skilful in his particular line of endeavor; he becomes a more accomplished musician, a more creative artist, a more imaginative inventor, a more expert mathematician. Except in the rare cases of those who are chosen to be world teachers, these individuals are left in the world to show by their example of selflessness what it means to be "in the world but not of it"—to lead an active, interesting, creative, and profitable life and still not seek selfishly for gain, for reputation, for glory. There are spiritually illumined men and women everywhere who are quietly and efficiently continuing their work as doctors, lawyers, inventors, manufacturers, et cetera, but showing that they can deal fairly, honestly, and generously with their employees and associates without suffering any loss to themselves. It is these men and women who are now exemplifying rightful and peaceful human relationships among all men.

As we pause for a while in these peaceful and hallowed surroundings, it is very easy to love one another in complete disregard of race, color, creed, religious or political differences. But it is not a simple matter to maintain this state of consciousness out in the world where the desire for personal benefit and gain is evident at every hand. That is why it is so very important and necessary that those who receive some measure of the spiritual light remain in the world for the time being, carrying this relationship into the realm of business, art, government—thereby showing by their example that we are all brothers and sisters through the common bond of our spiritual natures; that we have but one Father; that we have but one God. We must exemplify that we can carry this relationship into the outside world, so that the day will come when every man and woman will bend their knees to this spiritual wisdom and love.

There is a grace of God that has been at work in our consciousness through countless generations to lead us to this present day. We have not come here by accident nor by choice. You have not chosen this day, nor have I. This day was chosen by God. The divine grace operated in each one to bring us together in this certain place on this certain day. And just in case you might think that this wonderful light which we are sharing today is benefiting only those who are gathered together in this Ashram, I will tell you a little known secret: every word that is being spoken here is being heard throughout the world, wherever a spiritually attuned man or woman is listening. God never does anything just for you or for me alone. The work of God is for all people of good will who are opening themselves to truth. You may be surprised some day to learn that in America, in

Canada, in England, in South Africa, and in many other places all the blessings that we are enjoying here were also known and enjoyed there. Our example of spiritual brotherhood and love is but a tiny little bit of a stone dropped into the waters of human consciousness, the circles of which will spread around the world.

Every spiritual impulse that takes place in the consciousness of a master is felt in the consciousness of all those who are attuned to the Spirit. That is how the master draws his students unto himself —the light in the consciousness of the master is felt in the consciousness of the student. Thus it is that every Godly thought that is in your consciousness or mine today is being felt somewhere by someone who is spiritually attuned. Somewhere a sick person suddenly is restored to health; somewhere an accident is averted; somewhere a sinner is cleansed— only because a ray of the pure spiritual light of God was received in your consciousness and in mine.

Never must we think that we are limited, or that the good we can do is limited. We must understand that we are instruments or channels through which God reaches others of His children. From your own experience, you know that your master is the channel through whom the love of God comes to you. In like manner, in some measure every spiritual impulse received by you goes out to benefit and bless others, and to bring about the glorious day when the entire world will be united in the realization of oneness. There is a bond that unites us and which also unites all of our brothers and sisters of the world with us. This bond is love. It is this spiritual bond of love for God, love for our master, and love for each other that will achieve our ultimate spiritual freedom.

Never can there be freedom on earth until there is spiritual freedom in the individual. Never will one be free through war or conquest. Never will one be free until freedom first is felt in the Soul. This is the true basis of religion—the wonderful teaching of the East that has made its way through the West and once again returns to pay homage to its masters.

Reprinted from *The Vision*, February, 1956.
Anandashram P.O., Kanhangad, South India

CHAPTER EIGHT

CONTEMPLATIVE MEDITATION

The Middle Path

Why callest thou me good? there is none good
but one, that is, God.

Matthew 19:17

THE universe of God's creating is within us. God's
love permeates, enfolds, and upholds this universe
and all that is therein. All that exists is of God, and
God is the good unto us and unto all creation. This
is a spiritual universe, and in it there is nothing good
nor evil. Let us make this lesson a meditation,
whereby we prepare ourselves to be receptive and
responsive to the experience of good by admitting
God into our undivided consciousness. Let us close
our eyes to appearances and open our Souls to Spirit,
acknowledging God to be the only good, and realizing
that all that exists partakes of God's goodness.

Heretofore, we have lived in a world of two powers.
In vain we have endeavored to invoke a good power
to escape or overthrow an evil power. Now we will
do neither. We will rest content *in that which is*,
and by translating any appearance or suggestion
into that which *it is*, we will behold harmony,
health, completeness, and wholeness even where discord and disease profess to be. We will rest in the
realization that there is no power apart from God;

that God's omnipresence, omnipotence, omniscience is the assurance that good pervades all being, all form, all effect. We will withhold all judgment and opinion as to good and evil and acknowledge that God alone is good. This calls for a rebirth on the part of each one of us. It means that we are to agree within ourselves that in all this world of persons and conditions God alone is good, and that God's goodness permeates and pervades all that exists. There is no evil because God, infinite good, has not created evil, and there is no other creator.

If we have entertained an evil sense of person or condition, let us purify ourselves of such beliefs by realizing that no quality of evil, no power of evil exists; that regardless of what may be presenting itself in the way of harmony or discord is neither good nor evil, for *only God is*. If we walk through the valley of the shadow of death, and though we may seem to be consumed by disease, we will have no fear for, in and of themselves, they possess no causative factor of destruction, no element of death. Since all power is in God, they are nothingness. We will not say of these appearances that they are good or that they are evil—merely that they are nothingness. God is allness. Appearances are nothingness. God's allness, God's goodness, God's power, and God's law permeate this universe, all conditions, and all being.

Beholding good and evil is a state of duality, so keep foremost the truth that nothing, in and of itself, is either good or evil. However, a person, thing, circumstance, or condition becomes good or evil in proportion to your thinking or believing it so, so that something that may seem very good to you is evil to your neighbor; and what might appear as good to your neighbor seems evil to you. Your own way of thinking can make a thing good or bad in your experience, not as a reality but as an illusion which will seem very real if you entertain such thoughts.

"There is nothing from without a man, that entering into him can defile him: but the things which come out of him, those are they that defile the man." One's life experience is composed of that which emanates from one's own consciousness. Therefore, never again can the inharmonies of your lives be ascribed to persons or conditions, because now you realize that nothing that man can do and nothing that goes into your experience defileth or maketh a lie; but, rather, that which emanates from your own consciousness determines your experience. If you persistently live in the world of duality by considering some things good and some evil you are casting the bread of duality upon the waters and, invariably, that bread of duality will return to you.

The old proverb, "As a man thinketh, so is he," does not mean what he thinks in his mind exactly, but what he thinks in his heart—whatever he is convinced of within himself, whatever he entertains in consciousness is what he draws unto himself. Therefore, if you entertain no awareness or consciousness or sense of evil none can react upon you. Cast upon the waters your understanding of oneness, the awareness of God's grace as your sufficiency, your recognition of God as the all Good, and these will return to you.

The belief of evil which you entertain in your own consciousness is the only evil that can react upon you. ". . . for whatsoever a man soweth, that shall he also reap." If you permit your consciousness to be occupied by a sense of evil, that sense of evil returns to harm your being, your body, your business. By relinquishing all sense of evil, and refusing to invest anything with such so-called power, your consciousness is cleansed and there is no longer any evil to operate in or upon you.

Evil has no existence regardless of any appearance of discord that may be evident at this moment. That which we have been fearing and hating and dreading is not evil, because God is all, and God is good. This understanding will lead us out of the age-old belief of a power of God and a power of devil, a power of immortal mind and a power of mortal mind, into the fourth dimensional consciousness, which consciousness acknowledges that *all that is* receives its power, substance, cause, and law from God. Wonders of grace come into our experience in proportion as we withdraw judgments, theories, beliefs, labels, and terms from the world of persons and things and no longer speak a language of comparisons. Begin now by discarding all such ideas suggested by human sense in the understanding and recognition that God is the one causative Principle and that, therefore, this universe and all that is in it is spiritual.

God's grace reveals that never has there been discord or disease or death in all of creation, but because we have accepted the world's concept of good and evil that is what we have demonstrated.

But now, as we advance into spiritual enlightenment, we will desist from labelling anything evil, and we will cease to believe that any condition possesses power of evil, pain, or destruction, because all power emanates from God. We will no longer believe in a law of disease, since all law is of God. There are no laws of opposites—there is only one law, one spiritual law, good, which governs God's creation. Since God made all that is made, there is no other creation. "God saw every thing that he had made, and, behold, it was very good." Therefore, we must not be deceived and tempted by appearances to say this is error, that is discord, and proceed to attempt to rid ourselves of it or rise above it. We must come into the realization that God made all that was made, and all that was made is maintained and sustained by its creative Principle. This spiritual perception will result in translating these false appearances into the vision of the divine harmony which is ever present.

As you retire into the depths of your own consciousness where all terms of a human designation are relinquished, you become aware of God alone, and you will behold the vision of God's spiritual perfection and goodness upholding, sustaining, maintaining, and keeping His spiritual universe in perfect peace and eternal harmony. "The heavens declare the glory of God; and the firmament sheweth his handywork."

*   *   *

Therefore if thou bring thy gift to the altar, and there rememberest that thy brother hath aught against thee; Leave there thy gift before the altar, and go thy way; first be reconciled to thy brother, and then come and offer thy gift.

Matthew 5:23, 24

If, at any time, you attempt to pray or commune with God and remember that you are holding varying concepts of good and evil—stop right there and make peace within yourself by agreeing that only God is good, and that the infinity of God's goodness leaves nothing of an evil or destructive nature. When you stand in the Presence in spiritual purity, no longer at war within yourself against any person, any thing, or any condition, coming to the Father with clean hands, having naught against anyone, entertaining no false concepts, and accepting nothing as evil—at peace with all creation—then you may return to your prayer.

The grace of God is enabled to flow in a consciousness that is not divided and at war, that is single-pointed and single-eyed, that acknowledges one Presence, one Power, with no opposites and no opposition. In this undefiled state of spiritual purity the grace of God pervades, overspreads, and fills your mind, your body, your Soul, your very being. Then is prayer answered. But while we live in a dual world wherein we believe someone or something possesses qualities or propensities of good or evil we are a state of consciousness at war—a house divided against itself—and the grace of God cannot reveal itself in such a divided household. We must be of a single mind, we must see with a single eye, and to do that we must withdraw all labels of good and evil, and acknowledge all good to be of God—for God alone is good.

We must continue to be in the world, but not of it. We must continue to care for the affairs of our family, social, and business life, as well as community, national, and international life—but while doing so we must not accept the world's standards. We must be above all such concepts, and we must stand back and realize that inherent in all this universe there is no power or property of evil whatsoever. Make it a daily practice to go to the altar with a consciousness free of enmity, free of beliefs of evil powers, evil presences, evil conditions, evil potentialities. Bring unto God a consciousness purified with the understanding that God alone is good; that God's goodness is the truth of individual being, individual conditions, individual thoughts, individual things; that there is no other power, no other law. Then your prayer reaches the throne of heaven, the very center of your being, and the entire universe is enfolded in God's grace.

There is only one truth, and that is God. Therefore, to behold evil in any way is to behold evil in God. There is no evil. There is only an infinity of good, an eternality of good—God, the all Good, is the only truth. Purge consciousness of the belief in appearances that testify to two powers and recognize only one Power—God, infinite Good. As you behold the Christ as the reality of every individual, the substance, law, and activity of every condition, you hold no duality in your consciousness, and none can return to you. In proportion as this truth is active in your consciousness you are truly master of your fate and captain of your Soul.

There is no power and no law capable of opposing the value of 2×2; there is no power and no law capable of setting aside the harmony of do, re, mi. These quantities and qualities are intact and unchangeable, without opposition, governed by immutable laws which are maintained and sustained unto eternity. This is true of every man, woman, and child on earth. There is no power to destroy the perfection and harmony of our being. There is no opposition to immortality and eternality. A dual mind has led us to believe in two powers, but now, in this day of purification, we return to our Father's house, where we see as God sees. In this consciousness we are too pure to behold iniquity, because we are beholding with Christ consciousness—the consciousness of God. We do not believe that there is an evil person, thing, condition, power, or propensity in this entire universe. This consciousness is the mind that was in Christ Jesus. When that mind said, to what appeared as a cripple, "Arise, take up thy bed, and go into thine house," it recognized no condition apart from God—it saw neither a well body nor a diseased body—it saw only the body which is God.

No individual possesses any personal qualities of goodness—nor any personal qualities of evil. But every individual possesses Christhood—God-ness, God-being—that pure state of consciousness in which there are no opposites and no opposition. We are too pure to behold two powers, one good and one evil; two substances, one spiritual and one material. Through the mind that was in Christ

Jesus, we behold the vision of one Power, one Presence, and that One, God.

It has taken long and arduous generations to meet the discords and inharmonies of human sense because we have persistently entertained a sense of a selfhood apart from God by accepting the belief that there is someone or something from which we must gain freedom. As long as we prolong that state of consciousness we cannot be free in Christ. Here we must make a definite distinction: never seek to be free *from* any person or condition, because, in so doing, veritably you set up the duality. *Seek freedom in Christ!* Never seek freedom from the world. Seek freedom in Christ—in the awareness that you *are* free in Christ; that Christ is the life that permeates your being in harmony, health, completeness, and perfection; that Christ is the liberty wherewith you are clad. Realize this freedom in Christ as the perfection of spiritual being. "Stand fast therefore in the liberty wherewith Christ hath made us free, and be not entangled again with the yoke of bondage."

Freedom is a quality enjoyed when we have overcome duality by refusing to entertain any sense of iniquity or destruction, or beliefs in a presence or power apart from God. We are clothed and in our right mind when we are clad with the liberty of the Sons of God. As long as there is a sense of duality in an individual's consciousness he is subject to the discords of the world, but they will not come nigh the dwelling place of one who dwelleth in the "secret place of the most High"—in Christ consciousness. Realize freedom in the oneness of consciousness in which there is no presence or power opposed to God. Freedom is in and of Christ—it is never to be obtained from any one or any thing.

No man is a healer, nor can any man become a healer, but every man can reveal God's grace, harmony, and peace governing and maintaining this universe—in just the same way that the mathematician corrects the belief that 2×2 equals 5 by knowing that 2×2 equals 4. The mathematician changes nothing, corrects nothing, except the erroneous premise—because 2×2 is never other than 4. We do not heal—we simply rectify the erroneous belief that there is someone or something to be healed by correcting the concept that there are two powers operating in the experience of the world. In this correct understanding we acknowledge God's law alone operating in all of creation.

As we quietly ponder and consider this great spiritual truth we are experiencing a distinct form of meditation, but one that includes much more than the word implies. It is communion with, and in, Truth; it is prayer; and it is treatment. We may apply any of these terms, but, actually, the highest connotation is that of contemplative meditation, wherein we have shut out the world of persons and things by contemplating the nature of Truth as one. In this meditation, in which we contemplate Truth as power, there is no such thing as evil power. As we contemplate Truth as substance, there is no other substance to be overcome or destroyed. In this meditation no lie can enter to violate the truth of oneness. This contemplative meditation of God's grace and goodness is the prayer that results in realization, whereby that which we have been contemplating becomes real and demonstrable. It is for this reason that we may also call it treatment. During this period of contemplation and reflection, there comes a moment of complete silence in which we wait upon the Lord—"Speak, Lord: for thy servant heareth," and as we wait in this silence, from the very depths of our innermost being there comes the unmistakable certainty of God's presence—a feeling that this that we have declared and acknowledged is true! In this sacred and holy state we have realized prayer, realized treatment, realized meditation—realized *God*! Never be content, however, merely to let the act of meditation, contemplation, prayer, or treatment suffice. Never be satisfied until you have actually turned to the Father within and, after relaxing in the everlasting arms, listened and waited until the seal is placed upon it.

Contemplative meditation is a holy sacrament and should never be discussed even among one's closest spiritual friends. Keep it sacred and secret until such time as it becomes such a positive conviction and realization that you are able to demonstrate it in bringing forth harmonies in your own existence and to those around you. Then it speaks for itself, and reveals itself to others.

This Middle Path is the highest revelation of the Master's teaching, and one which even only a few of the disciples were able to comprehend, so do not attempt to teach or demonstrate it until it has become your own. Because of the depth of this truth it has been lost to the world, because it is difficult and almost impossible to accept in the face of appearances which are always testifying to the opposites of good and evil, poverty and wealth, sickness and health, life and death. Perhaps even some who are reading these words (with the exception of students of serious and positive intent) will find it difficult to believe that absolutely no one and no thing in all this universe possesses an evil power, capacity, or propensity. This spiritual perception and discernment is achieved through inner reflection, contemplation, and meditation upon all these truths, whereby the principle of one Power, Good, is revealed from within your individual being. Some of you have only my word for it; some have only a few pages of scripture or statements of truth as their basis; some are a step further and have an inner feeling that this is true—but that is not enough. Just as Mary took the Babe down into Egypt where it was hidden for a year, so must you take this truth into your consciousness and hide it, ponder it, meditate upon it, until the time when your own Soul says, "This is the truth." When that day of inner realization dawns you will behold that even in this objectified world it is true. Then, and only then, can you begin the mission of revealing this truth to whoever may be receptive to it.

Again we must speak a word of caution: do not, under any circumstances, give this great truth to the unprepared thought! Never discuss or argue truth. Truth does not lend itself to reason: either one feels the rightness of it or he does not, and, if not, one is not ready for the experience. ". . . the natural man (that is, the unprepared thought) receiveth not the things of the Spirit of God: for they are foolishness unto him: neither can he know them, because they are spiritually discerned." The Master was well aware of the unbelieving and skeptical thought, for he once remarked, ". . . neither will they be persuaded, though one rose from the dead." We have all witnessed that until a person is prepared to receive spiritual vision, he will not even accept the healing of a disease or discord as an actual demonstration of truth. Therefore, if you feel the rightness of this truth, keep it within yourself—treasure it as you would cherish a precious gem, and share it discreetly only with those who appreciate gems.

The evidence of the senses tells us that sin, disease, lack, limitation, and death are detrimental and destructive powers. But this truth I now give to you: there is no power, either of good or evil, in anyone, in any thing, or in any effect. All power is in God, and that power is good. It was this vision of one Power, in which he beheld a spiritual universe governed, maintained, and sustained by the grace of God, in which there was no evil to be overcome, no disease to be healed, no sinner to be reformed, no death to fear, that enabled the Master to stand fearless before Pilate, and say, "Thou couldest have no power at all against me, except it were given thee from above." And when he said, "Peace I leave with you, my peace I give unto you: not as the world giveth, give I unto you," he was telling us, in effect: "The peace of my undivided consciousness, which is of the household of God, possessing only the qualities and attributes of God, peopled only with the children of God—*that* peace

I give unto you." As you entertain this divine idea, this spiritual truth of oneness, you also will find that the power and peace of an undivided household will descend upon you—"And the peace of God, which passeth all understanding, shall keep your hearts and minds through Christ Jesus."

Be Taught of God

Now we have received, not the spirit of the world, but the spirit which is of God; that we might know the things that are freely given to us of God. Which things also we speak, not in the words which man's wisdom teacheth, but which the Holy Ghost teacheth; comparing spiritual things with spiritual.

I Corinthians 2:12, 13

Between the spiritual teacher and student there is a reciprocal spark of receptivity and responsiveness, because always the teacher has something to share which the student cannot obtain in any other way. The truth of God must be imparted only to the children of God—to those of one's own household, to those of one's own state of consciousness—for only such can receive it. That is why the message of The Infinite Way is suitable for teaching or sharing with those who seek it, but cannot be given to the public at large. Paul tells us that ". . . the natural man receiveth not the things of the Spirit of God: for they are foolishness unto him: neither can he know them, because they are spiritually discerned."

Because of the fact that people are of vastly

different and varying states and stages of consciousness, it is impossible for any one individual to present the truth for the entire world. In this connection it is important that we realize this: all cannot receive Jesus Christ. There are those to whom the teachings of Buddha, Lao-tse, and Shankara are acceptable; others to whom the Hebrew prophets present the truth; and others to whom The Infinite Way and other modern teachings point the way to spiritual attainment. Scripture tells us, ". . . they shall be all taught of God," and ultimately each one will find his own teacher. Then it is that nothing can separate two such souls that have been united from a higher sphere in this state of spiritual consciousness.

We all have witnessed spiritual healing as it has been brought forth by The Infinite Way and other teachings, and always the source is the same. The principle is this: that since God is infinite, God is the only power. Therefore, what the world calls sin and disease *are not power*! If they *were* power, sin and disease could not be overcome. The only reason they exist in human consciousness is because, ever since the time of Adam, there has prevailed a universal belief in two powers—good and evil. Sometimes the words we use to discuss healing seem rather in the way of a contradiction or concession to the Bible, because there it appears that there is a power called God which does heal sin and disease. It is when you contact the realm of Spirit that you find this is not true—there are not two powers, because there are no opposites in Spirit. Once you realize your oneness with God, you discover there is no power with which disease can be healed, because you will find no disease to heal. Healing is merely a "Suffer it to be so now," to demonstrate God's harmony on earth.

The healing gift consists of a state of consciousness which recognizes and acknowledges only one Power, God; and which knows there is no power in sin and disease. It is when you open your inner Self to that which *is*, permitting *Is* to fill your consciousness, as you become aware of it in meditation, that the appearances of sin and disease dissolve and fade away. There have been other masters who showed forth healing, but it was this *knowing and awareness of one Power* that enabled Jesus to reveal it in its fullness.

Aside from his healing ministry Jesus was given another and greater work, and that was to reveal the kingdom of heaven on earth. By his healings Jesus proved that God was speaking and acting through him, and never before nor since has there been such an exposition of witnessing God in action. To some degree, in the days immediately following, the disciples were able to carry it on. Jesus' teaching mission was much more important than the healing, however. So also, the major ministry of The Infinite Way is not healing but teaching, and letting the healings accompany the teaching. The harvest is ripe but the laborers are few, and so what is most needed are students who can teach as well as heal.

The ministry of Christ is universal and is being brought to light through many avenues. It is this that will leaven the human scene until, eventually, there will be a day when no one needs healing. Once, when the seventy joyously returned from a healing mission, they said to the Master, "Lord, even the devils are subject unto us through thy name." But the Master, with great understanding and compassion, replied, "Notwithstanding in this rejoice not, that the spirits are subject unto you; but rather rejoice, because your names are written in heaven." In other words, rejoice not in the healing itself, but rejoice that you are spiritual and already perfect; rejoice that there is but one Power, and therefore there is no one and no condition to be healed. God does not give us power over evil. Rather, God reveals that we are His children, and with that revelation there is no need for healing, *because the Son of God never needs healing!*

"These things I have spoken unto you, that in me ye might have peace. In the world ye shall have tribulation: but be of good cheer; I have overcome the world." When the Master spoke these words, he meant that he had overcome the illusion of this world. "These things I have spoken unto you, that in me ye might have peace"—by which he meant spiritual peace—the Christ-peace, the peace that has no qualities, no degrees, but is always at the standpoint of perfection. There are no discords in heaven, and once the Christ-peace is accepted in consciousness there is no more need for healing, for we will have realized that sin, disease, lack, limitation, and death are not powers and have no place in God's kingdom. Yes, even death will be overcome, for there will be no conditions leading to death.

"I have overcome the world." What is this *I* that performs such a miracle? *I am that I am.*

Where is this *I*? *I am* within you—closer than breathing, nearer than hands and feet. "I am with you alway, even unto the end of the world. . . . I have meat to eat that ye know not of . . . the water that I shall give him shall be in him a well of water springing up into everlasting life. . . . I am the bread of life: he that cometh to me shall never hunger; and he that believeth on me shall never thirst. . . . I am the way, the truth, and the life." The Lord thy God in the midst of you will never leave you, nor forsake you, and is available every day of your life as you cease struggling and fearing and retire into quiet, confident, and grateful communion with the Father, in the realization that the allness of the kingdom of God is within you.

The greatest healing principle in the world is to be able to recognize and rely on the *I* that is within you. When you come into this realization your work will be a work of love, for *I am* fulfilment. All good flows to the individual who learns the password *I*, and nothing of a discordant nature can come nigh the dwelling place of one who understands its profound meaning. Take this understanding of *I* into the secret chambers of your being, remembering always that it is only what you know in secret that can be shouted from the housetops. If you pray in public you will receive the approval of men, but if you pray and commune and show forth your love of God in secret you will be rewarded by your Father who heareth in secret. Who is your Father? *I am!*

Let your prayer be: "Thank you, Father: *I am.* The kingdom of God is within me." In this communion with the inner Self, the divine *I*, you need not pray for any thing, for it is the Father's good pleasure to give you the Kingdom. You have only to accept the abundant blessings that are continuously pouring out to you and through you. In this communion, ask only for awakening, understanding, and light—that you may be taught of the Holy Ghost, and that you may "know the things that are freely given to us of God."

What Is Religion?

The following is the text of my second talk given to devotees of Anandashram, on December 9th, 1955:

We have learned that religion had its beginning in India and spread out from India to the East and to the West. Now we ask: What is religion? What is the religion that was given to us in the beginning, when the hearts and Souls of men opened themselves to God for light?

The study of the many scriptures that comprise our spiritual literature reveals that religion is a release—a release from the limitations of humanhood into God awareness. Even today, religion should be understood as a release from our mortal selfhood and our material sense of life into an expanded universe-consciousness, God consciousness, spiritual consciousness.

In the next order was revealed the way—yes, the term is "the way"—the way to be freed of the limitations of sinful desires, physical, mental, and moral sicknesses, financial lack. But how is one to be free of these, and how is one to be expanded into an awareness of God's abundance? The secret is this: it is God's abundance that becomes our experience. Really, it is God's life that is realized as our life. It is God's abundant supply that becomes our individual supply. It is God's love that is shown forth as our love for each other. The way is through prayer, for prayer is our means of contact with our infinite Source.

Prayer has many forms. Probably, the easiest form for the youngest students to understand is a prayer of words, spoken silently within or audibly without. This is the voice of our own heart speaking to our concept of God, and very often the heart is unburdened as we speak to God with words. Later, prayer ascends to thoughts—unspoken thoughts instead of words. In our periods of silence we learn to speak with God silently, with thoughts of communion, thoughts of joy, thoughts of peace.

From these two simple beginnings, prayer continues to ascend until, through meditation, eventually prayer becomes an absolute silence, in which and through which the voice of God reaches and speaks to us. No longer do we speak to God; no longer do we think up to God; but, rather, in the silence, God speaks to us, guides and leads us, and reveals Himself to us.

In these many centuries since religion was revealed to man's consciousness, prayer has taken many wrong turns, until a great deal of prayer, both in the East and in the West, is now perverted, turned into wrong channels, and becomes a means of selfishness. That is why we find the world today in chaos, in discord, in inharmony. Too many prayers are merely asking and beseeching God for blessings for me, my family, and my nation. These prayers can never be answered, because God is Love, and God does not love one more than another, nor does God benefit one at the expense of another. And so, until prayer becomes the unselfish realization of God's universal goodness, prayer continues unanswered and darkness remains. Darkness remains in the consciousness of the individual and in the consciousness of the world, and that darkness then interferes with human affairs.

The enlightened prayer of God realization dispels that darkness in the mind and body, in the home and nation. Enlightened prayer must always be a turning to the inner divine Self for revelation of *its light*, that this light may dispel our sense of separateness. When we pray: "Give us bread, give us freedom, give us health, give us wealth," the darkness only deepens. But when we pray: "Give us light—let Thy light be revealed," there follows, even in the very earliest stages of such enlightened prayer, a most wonderful revelation. A message is received which says, either in these words or in this sense: "God's grace is thy sufficiency!" Through this we realize that our only prayer need be: "Let Thy grace—Thy grace alone—be revealed, that Thy grace may become evident as peace in the mind and heart and Soul, and peace in human affairs."

Without doubt, one of the happiest days that ever comes to an individual is when he first realizes that God's grace is all he will ever need. Grace *is* our only need. Although we think we have need of food and clothing, through grace it is revealed that man shall not live by bread alone, and even the lilies of the field are clothed. We need only the realization of God's grace, and when grace descends upon us we are abundantly provided and lovingly cared for.

It has taken many centuries and the devotion of countless saints and seers to bring the world back, in this twentieth century, to where it was in the very beginning when it was first revealed that God's grace was a sufficiency for all our needs. Today, in many parts of the world, there are enlightened individuals who are turning the thought of people away from praying for things and conditions to the prayer of realization of God's grace as a sufficiency in all things. It is these few to whom the world will look for guidance and direction in this enlightened prayer, until such time as the world itself comes into an understanding of the true nature of prayer.

Harmony of body and supply, harmony of family life, and harmony of national and international life are the natural unfoldments of God realization. It is no more necessary to pray specifically for help than it is to pray for sunshine. It is no more necessary to pray for supply and abundance than it is to pray for potatoes to produce potatoes or for rice to produce rice. Always there is in operation the law of like begetting like: from the rose shall come roses, and from the cow shall come cows. Already there is in operation a law that day must follow night and night must follow day. One need not pray for these things—merely become aware that God's grace is the law, and God's law is love. It is because of this law of love that the tides turn on schedule, that the stars are in the appointed places on time, that the sun and moon and earth maintain their positions. The universe is maintained and sustained by God's law of love, and in just this same manner does God's law of love care and provide for every child of God, be he human or animal, vegetable or mineral. But this we must understand and remember: this law and this love only operate for us as we, individually, open ourselves to God's grace.

The Western world often asks the question: If the religion originated and given to the world by the East is the true religion, why has the East suffered and endured such hardships in the last centuries? It also asks: If there is a great God of divine love, the Father-God of whom Jesus taught, why do the Western nations undergo a ceaseless succession of disease, dissension, strife, and war? To both questions the answer is the same: God *is*; God's goodness *is*; God's grace *is*; but it is only operative in our experience in proportion to the degree of our acceptance and realization of this truth. For example, if we were to lock ourselves in a room with all the blinds drawn, we would sit in darkness without benefit of the light and warmth of the sun outside. In the same manner, if we draw the blinds against the Spirit, the grace of God cannot infiltrate and penetrate the darkness of human sense. In order to achieve harmony in our individual and collective affairs, it is necessary that we open consciousness to permit the entrance of God, not by seeking to get something from God, but by giving something of God to our fellow-men.

God is the source of all good. In our spiritual

Selfhood, we are the children of God, heirs to all the heavenly riches, and it is God's pleasure to give us the kingdom. To God we can give nothing, but we can accept the grace that flows so abundantly, and we can open out a way for it to flow to others. We must accept this grace, not only for ourselves, but for all.

It is sometimes believed that the health of the body and mind is something different from the health of the Soul, but it is not. When the Soul is at peace, the body responds and shows forth this peace. The Soul is our real being, and the action of the Soul operates in our body to give health and strength, in our business to give guidance, direction, and prosperity, and in our nations to give wisdom, honor, and justice. The Soul is the source of all human good, and when we are in contact with the Soul-center, we do not find body and business and government things separate and apart, but we find that body and business and government are all acted upon by the Soul. When this contact with our inner Self is made, and when consciousness is filled with the realization of God's presence, all our earthly affairs respond.

The East seems to feel that the Western world pays too much attention to the body, to the accumulation of wealth and material possessions, and to mechanical and industrial progress. This is true only where health or wealth or progress is the prime goal. When bodily health and material wealth assume too great an importance, they become obstructions to spiritual development. But when spiritual development and the realization of the Soul-capacities becomes the sole aim, it automatically follows that the so-called human affairs respond to the spiritual impulse and become harmonious.

When the young student first turns to God, usually it is because of a desire for better health or greater wealth, but soon he finds that these cannot be attained until he has achieved his spiritual contact with God. It is most marvelous to watch the beauties that are unfolded in his experience as God becomes the central theme, the first and greatest desire. The intent and purpose of prayer is not the attainment of harmony, but the attainment of God consciousness, spiritual consciousness, and when the heart sings with true prayer the effect is harmony in all our affairs of body and being. In this light, prayer becomes a very exciting and joyous experience, because in addition to the prayers in which we participate in temples and holy places, there are the prayers that continually sing within us as we go about our daily tasks. Then it is that we understand that it is not necessary to pray for help or for a specific good. It is only necessary that we open ourselves to receive the grace of God, and that we be willing to share this grace with those not yet aware of their divine heritage.

There is still a higher aspect to the subject of religion and prayer. In the West, most people are inclined to think of life merely as a period between the cradle and the grave, believing that this is the only life about which they need be concerned. In the religious world of the East, however, there is a greater recognition of the life which existed before the cradle, and of the life that exists beyond the grave. Devotion to religion and prayer eventually unfolds the knowledge and understanding that this present life can be, should be, and is, a preparation for the experience that lies before us, just as life before the cradle was an experience that brought us to the place we are today. Religion and prayer are the development of the Soul, not only for the harmony of everyday earthly living, but for the harmony and progress of our experience unto eternity. We must never lose sight of the fact that in God realization we perform two functions: we bring about peace and harmony in our present lives; and we bring the assurance of progress in our lives to come.

When we pray alone, often there is a great struggle to rise above the limitations of our personal sense of prayer. It is when we find an enlightened Soul that our ideas and capacities for prayer are expanded, and the way is opened that frees us from these limitations and more quickly enables us to enter the kingdom of God on earth. It is in this way that we receive help, not only in our everyday affairs, but the greater help that opens the consciousness of our Soul to the ability to realize God. For every individual on earth there is a teacher, visible or invisible, and the first prayer of every student and seeker of truth should be that he be led to that teacher; and once finding him to accept the grace which comes through the heart and Soul of such an enlightened one.

Prayer is an important part of life, second only to the subject of religion itself, and yet the two are inseparable. The life of prayer reveals the life of

God as man's individual life. In the West, to a great extent, prayer is confined to Sunday or other specific days, but more and more it is beginning to be understood that prayer must be without ceasing —twenty-four hours of every day, seven days a week. There was a time when everyone who embarked upon a life of prayer left his household and entered a temple, a monastery, or convent; but now it is known that a life of prayer can be lived right where we are, in the midst of home, business, and government demands. Spiritual men and women are called by God, and when life is lived in an unceasing atmosphere of prayer, those few individuals who have been chosen to be spiritual leaders will be lifted out of their everyday lives. But never should one be encouraged or even consider leaving his human surroundings until the call is unmistakable. Only in this way will the spiritual men and women of the world be worthy of their calling. When this is thoroughly understood there will no longer be false prophets and false teachers, nor will people leave the human world for what they consider the spiritual world before they are called. It also will be understood that each individual is called to fulfill some specific spiritual function in the divine plan; therefore there will be no lack, no disease, no war, and no unhappiness; and every individual will be cared for physically, mentally, morally, and economically. There are those who must be saints and seers and spiritual teachers, just as there are those who must fill positions in the family, business, and government; but each one who fulfills any of these in the realization of his spiritual destiny fulfills it harmoniously, joyously, successfully; with love, generosity, and forgiveness.

The greatest privilege that can ever come to an individual is that of sharing the grace of God which is received and revealed in the silence and secrecy of the heart. The most sacred work on earth is the giving and sharing of God's riches of spiritual wisdom. My own heart is full of gratitude that God has spoken to me in silence, in sacredness, and in secrecy, and then permitted me to share these spiritual gems with others. One of the greatest human privileges that has ever been mine is the rare opportunity to travel to far places, and to encounter such enlightened souls as our beloved Swami Ramdas, who so liberally shared his spiritual gems as he travelled the world last year. I am sure Swami Ramdas knows my great joy in being permitted to speak on these occasions at Anandashram. To all of you, may I say that you have given me far more than I have been permitted to give you—more in spiritual memories than I will be able to store up in the next three or four lifetimes.

Reprinted from *The Vision*, April, 1956, Anandashram P.O., Kanhangad, South India

CHAPTER NINE

SPIRITUAL ILLUMINATION
THE WAY OF HARMONY

THERE is one reason for the individual and collective discords of this world—only one reason why anyone is sinful, sick, or poor; only one reason why nations contend and wage war against each other. That reason is material sense—limitation, finiteness, the belief that matter is a reality, and that matter constitutes all there is to the world. Material sense would have us believe we have a physical body that has only so many years to function. Material sense says that the world contains so many square miles of land and so many dollars, and four billion people are struggling to divide it. It is material sense that makes one desire what another possesses, to the extent that men are willing to steal and cheat and even kill to obtain it.

The foundation of our spiritual work is set forth in the following quotation from *The Infinite Way*[1]:

Illumination dissolves all material ties and binds men together with the golden chains of spiritual understanding; it acknowledges only the leadership of the Christ; it has no ritual or rule but the divine, impersonal universal Love; no

[1] By Joel S. Goldsmith (San Gabriel, Calif.: Willing Publishing Company, 1956) p. 40.

other worship than the inner Flame that is ever lit at the shrine of Spirit. This union is the free state of spiritual brotherhood. The only restraint is the discipline of Soul, therefore we know liberty without license; we are a united universe without physical limits; a divine service to God without ceremony or creed. The illumined walk without fear—by Grace.

Such illumined spiritual consciousness reveals that we need nothing of each other, because "All things that the Father hath are mine."

The nations of the world will heartily agree that this is a beautiful, idealistic, and much to be desired theory, but not for one moment will they believe it to be practical. The practicality and usability of the Christ teaching never will be known, or understood, or demonstrated by man whose breath is in his nostrils, because, to him, the only important thing is that there is a certain amount of money to be made, a certain amount of safety and security to be maintained, a certain amount of pleasure to be enjoyed, and his sole interest is in how he is to get his share of it. Spiritual consciousness cannot penetrate this density of material sense. That is why so many people fail to grasp it. They are so engrossed in indulging the driving ambitions and pleasures of humanhood that there exists no room for spiritual consciousness until, as ofttimes happens, they find themselves so plunged into trouble that the very desperation of the situation forces them to give up the fraudulent material sense and open themselves to God.

The Master taught that we must not be like the nations of the world, seeking what we shall eat and drink, or how we shall be clothed; but that *we*, his disciples and students, *must seek the kingdom of God.* He goes even further: "Sell that ye have, and give alms; provide yourselves bags which wax not old, a treasure in the heavens that faileth not, where no thief approacheth, neither moth corrupteth. For where your treasure is, there will your heart be also." It is futile to tell an unbelieving world to take no thought for its life, and that all it must do in order to be prosperous is to give. How can one live except by hard work, elaborate planning, and clever scheming? How can one prosper or accumulate wealth by sharing and giving it away? One becomes rich by taking and acquiring! Nevertheless, it is true—one experiences prosperity and abundance in proportion to his giving. Such truths are foolishness and meaningless to the nations of materialists because they do not comprehend the things of God. *However, the things of God can be demonstrated by individuals who perceive the nature of spiritual truth.* "Are ye so without understanding also. . . . Having eyes, see ye not? and having ears, hear ye not? and do ye not remember?" Only those individuals of spiritual vision who, by rising above the limitations of humanhood, have definitely and resolutely set their feet upon the spiritual path can recognize this truth, practice it, and, ultimately, demonstrate it.

The world must be awakened from its material sense, and who but the spiritually illumined can awaken it? None other can do it. As yet, no one individual has ever claimed that power, and it is doubtful that any ever will, but even one individual with some degree of spiritual consciousness can accomplish great things. However, the awakening cannot come about through the intellect, nor by preaching and repeating what has been learned from books, but through spiritual illumination, and through those enlightened men and women who show by their fruitage the greater measure of harmony that is brought forth in their experience. In time, the world will come to desire that which they have, even if, at first, it is only the loaves and fishes. Did not most of us come to a spiritual study seeking healing, supply, and companionship? But after attaining a few of these things, did we not find that they failed to come up to our expectations, and that they were not what we wanted after all? It was then we realized that what we really were seeking was the Cause, and not the effect!

The spiritually illumined are those individuals who no longer are seeking an effect called healing or supply or companionship, but who are seeking the realization of their oneness with God, secure in the knowledge that the Son of God, the Christ, is heir to all the heavenly riches. Those who will be instrumental in awakening the world will know and teach that one does not seek the kingdom of God for physical, mental, moral, or financial healing, but that one seeks solely for the experience of God. Actually, that is why nothing is quite so practical as spiritual wisdom. When you forget the object you are seeking, you find it added in abundance; but first must come the transcendental faith and inner conviction that enables one to give up the search for health, wealth, and harmony, in and of themselves, and receive and enjoy them only as those things which are included in the attainment of spiritual consciousness.

As students of The Infinite Way, our vision is on attaining that mind which was in Christ Jesus, thereby becoming aware of the Spirit of God within all being. With that vision you must count yourselves a part of The Infinite Way, a part of me, a part of all others who have found this a message of salvation; and you must be willing to enter the ranks of those who will carry it to the world. This will not be by membership in organizations, but by your spiritual support—through meditation, prayer, and realization; and by such human support as may help to carry this message to the far corners of the earth. No longer can we think merely in terms of seeking good only for ourselves, but we must be willing and eager to share this unfolding good. Otherwise we do not enter into the fullness of our own demonstration. It is a spiritual law that one must give before one can receive; and never can one hope to receive what he has not given. You are entitled to the product of your own consciousness, and you can rest assured that it will be multiplied and sent back— but first your bread of spiritual recognition, love and understanding, sharing and devotion, must be cast upon the waters of human consciousness.

All good is of God, and those who live in the consciousness of having all from God, but nothing of themselves, experience the unfailing flow of grace. The spiritual principle: "For unto every one that hath shall be given, and he shall have abundance," was unconditionally demonstrated by the Master when he fed the multitudes—there was enough for all and twelve baskets full left over. This was the secret of the widow's small cruse of oil—when she began to share what she had, it did not fail. In the awareness that "The earth is the Lord's and the fullness thereof," comes the remembrance of the Father's promise: "Son, thou art ever with me, and all that I have is thine." When you perceive this principle and begin to give of that which you have, you will experience the full and abundant return. "But from him that hath not shall be taken away even that which he hath," and so if you claim to have nothing, and act as though you have nothing, eventually you will lose the little you do have.

The truth of the message of The Infinite Way is not mine personally, nor is it yours: it is ours to develop and use and share; otherwise it will be lost to us. If one were given a talent for music or art and did not develop and use it, it would not be long before the ability to play or paint would be lost. In the same way, if one is given a storehouse of spiritual truth and grace and does not use and share it, soon it will wither. So it is important that you who are partaking and enjoying the benefits of the study of spiritual truth begin to spend what you have—yourselves, your time and effort and assistance, your prayers and meditations. Spiritual truth must touch and awaken the world, and this can be accomplished only through such spending.

So that you may actively participate in this awakening, I ask that each student dedicate one meditation period each day to the specific realization of the Christ, for it is only through this realization that material sense will be dispelled, thus preparing the way for the receptivity of spiritual consciousness.

Enlightened Prayer

It is our custom to make tape recordings of our lectures and class work, so that the lessons may be available for use by student groups. As I speak, the words are recorded on the tape simply because the line between the microphone and the recording apparatus is kept open. If that line were to be closed, not one word would be recorded.

Never before in history have the churches been so filled as they are today. Never has there been so much interest in books and studies dealing with prayer and spiritual living. The entire world is praying for peace and the good things of life, yet continuing to suffer and experience lack, disease, disaster, and war. Why is this so? Although the world prays and prays and prays, it has no open line to God, and it is for this reason that the greater portion of these prayers are unanswered. Here we are, praying with words and thoughts to a God who is "out there" somewhere, but there is no contact. This sense of separation is the experience of the prodigal son, and no matter how often and how ardently we pray the discords continue. Prayer is that which destroys material sense, but it is the prayer of *realization*, not the selfish and meaningless petitions that are uttered in the hope of obtaining, acquiring, or attaining some personal end, nor even the fervent prayers for peace and good will. Such prayers are wasted, because there is no contact with God.

During many years of study and teaching, I have found that when I make the contact with God prayer is fulfilled. As this contact is made, prayer takes a different form, and we do not pray in the sense of asking for anything, because then we realize that there is no necessity to take thought for our lives. Never will we attain the heights of spiritual wisdom until we come to that place where there is nothing to pray for. Nowhere is there any record of the Master's praying for health or supply. His life was the perfect exemplification of his teaching that "I and my Father are one," and that it is the Father's good pleasure to give us the kingdom. Every mystic who has made conscious contact with God has found that the continuous outflow of love to and from God has provided everything needful for his fulfilment.

The Infinite Way teaches that this contact is made through meditation. Although some students achieve meditation quickly, in most cases it takes considerable time and practice. Meditation is attainable by everyone, but it is necessary to set aside a number of short periods at intervals throughout the day and night, during which one quietly turns thought to God as much as to say: "Speak, Lord: for thy servant heareth." Open the line to God by maintaining a listening attitude for a few minutes, and then go on about your business. Do not look for a result, because it makes no difference whether you receive a response or not. Occasionally you may receive direct guidance, but never expect voices or visions—these are merely effects and are of no importance. It is only important that you open consciousness to God as many times as possible—"Here I am, Father: I wait upon Thee." Repeat this in an hour or two, and if you should awaken in the night be very still and again wait in this receptive and listening attitude.

As this line is kept open, soon you will become aware that something new has entered your life, and that for some unexplainable reason a greater degree of harmony is evident in your experience. This intangible something is the Spirit of God, the Word, in which you are abiding, and which you are permitting to abide in you. In the fifteenth chapter of John, once again we read the memorable words of the Master which must be repeatedly impressed upon our consciousness: "I am the vine, ye are the branches: He that abideth in me, and I in him, the same bringeth forth much fruit: for without me ye can do nothing. If a man abide not in me, he is cast forth as a branch, and is withered; and men gather them, and cast them into the fire, and they are burned. If ye abide in me, and my words abide in you, ye shall ask what ye will, and it shall be done unto you. Herein is my Father glorified, that ye bear much fruit; so shall ye by my disciples." Those who live entirely in the human and material sense are as withering branches, and although some maintain their mental and physical capacities longer than others, they are wasting and using up their energies and are not being renewed by the Spirit— the line is closed and they are cut off. It is through these brief moments of receptivity that the line is re-established, and the first thing you know the Spirit begins to flow, bringing physical, mental, moral, and financial regeneration.

The kingdom of God is within us, but it has no means of expression unless we make way for it to escape. Have you ever really stopped to realize that the allness of God—eternality, immortality, divine life and love, ideal companionships and family relationships, abundant supply, glowing health—all of this splendor is imprisoned within each one of us? But because we have been so busily engaged entreating and praying for these very things to come from some outside source we have not received what we ask for. Nothing is to be found outside your own being—all is to be found within, and it must be discovered and realized through this contact in meditation, whereby you open the way for the love, intelligence, health, and supply of God to flow.

As you practice this several times each day and night, you actually come to feel and know and recognize the very presence of God within you, and you will become increasingly aware that it is this Presence that destroys material sense and opens out the way for spiritual consciousness to be realized on earth. As you feel this Spirit within you, others also feel it—not only does it touch your individual lives, but it touches your friends and enemies, your nations, and your world. That is why healings often occur during lectures and classes: someone makes a conscious contact during that period, and those who are tuned in on an open line receive the benefits. Every time you experience a conscious realization of God, that realization is destroying and dispelling material sense for another. It may be someone near or far away, someone who is ill or in prison, but always, wherever there is a receptive sense, someone benefits by your realization of the presence of God. It is through such enlightened prayer on the part of each student that the way is opened enabling the blessings of the Christ to flow out to awaken the nations of the world.

Practicing the Presence

HENRY THOMAS HAMBLIN

The secret of harmonious living is the development of spiritual consciousness. In that consciousness, fear and anxiety disappear. Life becomes meaningful with fulfilment its keynote.

From morning to night we are faced with appearances which would make us believe that there is power in effect. That is why in a world so abundantly supplied with all forms of good— diamonds, pearls, silver, oil, vegetables, fish, fruit —people are still praying for supply. They believe that all these forms of good are supply, whereas supply is within them. These things are effects of supply but it is consciousness that is the source of supply. Supply is spiritual, an activity of consciousness. At first we may only intellectually agree with this; but the day will come when it will be spiritually discerned, and then we shall see that the world of supply is within, although it appears visible in the without.

The above paragraphs from *Practicing the Presence*, by Joel S. Goldsmith, state very simply that harmonious living is all a matter of consciousness. When we have the right consciousness, we do not *want* things, but we express the very things which formerly we sought for. So, instead of a change of circumstances, what the aspirant needs is a change of consciousness.

One of the most impressive chapters in this book, and probably the most practical, is the one entitled, "To Him that Hath." Our readers are doubtless familiar with the saying that we should start where we *are*, and use what we *have*. So many of us make the mistake of thinking that if we were somewhere else and our circumstances easier, we could get on better, and that if we were possessed of more capital or were blessed with more brains or greater ability we could make our life truly successful. And also, in the same way, if we lived in a more spiritual environment, and if we were spiritual geniuses, then we might become seers or saints. But, of course, this idea is quite wrong. We have to start where we are and use what we have. Again I quote:

Scripture tells the story of the widow who fed Elijah. Even though she had only a 'handful of meal in a barrel, and a little oil in a cruse'; she did not say that she had not enough to share, but she first made a little cake for Elijah before she baked one for her son and herself. 'And the barrel of meal wasted not, neither did the cruse of oil fail.' She had little, but she used what she had and let it flow out from her.

Our Lord's feeding of the multitude is another illustration of this spiritual principle. When Jesus was told that the hungry thousands had no food, He asked what food have ye, and they said, five barley loaves and two small fishes. Jesus did not say that such a small amount was insufficient, but He used it and blessed it and gave to the people. The food was multiplied and all the people were fed to repletion, and yet there were twelve baskets full of food left over.

We have to use that which we have; which means going forward in faith, trusting in God as the one and only source. We do not trust in man or our own cleverness, or our own "humanhood," or what the Old Testament terms "the arm of flesh," but trust entirely to the One Creative Spirit or Divine Life and Substance, our Father. Then, because we do so, we *know* through actual experience that "the barrel of meal shall not waste, neither shall the cruse of oil fail." The widow had only a handful of meal in a barrel, and a little oil in a cruse, and yet she did as she was told and made the cake for Elijah. "And she and he and all her house did eat many days." She had to make her venture of faith first, after which abundance flowed. We call this a miracle, but it was not so. It was simply the working of divine Law. There is always adequate supply for every need, but we have to trust the Law and act accordingly. Then it is that we see signs following. We have to make a venture of faith; we have to use what we have. When we go forward in faith and trust, a vacuum is created, and this is filled by divine Substance.

The spiritual consciousness is not only a forgiving consciousness; it is also a giving consciousness. It does not want to get, but only to give. It wants to give all it has, looking for no reward, and one who has reached this consciousness is never happy except when giving. Because we love God, we want to give to God. There is no self-sacrifice about such giving. It is our greatest joy to give. According to St. Paul, one of the sayings of Jesus was: "It is better to give than to receive." And Jesus said: "If ye continue in my word, then are ye my disciples indeed; and ye shall know the truth, and the truth shall make you free."

Speaking of meditation, the author says:

Continuous inner meditation, continuous reaching toward the center of our being, will eventually result in the experience of the Christ. In that moment we discover the mystery of spiritual living. We do not have to take thought for what we shall eat, what we shall drink, nor wherewithal we shall be clothed; we do not have to plan; we do not have to struggle. Only Christ can live our life for us, and we meet the Christ within ourselves in meditation. The degree to which we attain the experience or activity of Christ, of the presence of the Spirit of God in us, determines the degree of individual unfoldment.

When we have attained this realization of the Spirit of God in man through meditation, and abide in it, retire into the center of our being, day in and day out, so that we never make a move without its inner assurance; the activity of the Christ feeds us, supplies us, enriches us, heals us, and brings us into the fulness of life. Then, of a certainty, we know, 'I am come that they might have life, and that they might have it more abundantly.' "

Reprinted from *Science of Thought Review*, June, 1956. Chichester, Sussex, England

CHAPTER TEN

THE DEMONSTRATION OF GOD

NOTHING from outside your own being can be added to you. All truth abides within you. You are Self-complete in God.

There are, no doubt, many ways or methods of coming into an awareness of spiritual truth. For instance, if one were to retire from the world, spending months or perhaps years in unceasing meditation and prayer, gradually the truth would come forth and announce itself, and ultimately all the truth that has been disclosed since the dawn of civilization would be realized. But such a somber and ascetic approach is by no means necessary, for even in this modern day of worldly pressures and demands it is possible to come into this realization without leaving one's human surroundings and interests. One such way is by means of a devoted and consecrated study of spiritual wisdom, and, more especially, through contact with the consciousness of an illumined and enlightened teacher. Throughout the ages such a method or system of teaching has been in operation, whereby teachers with some measure of spiritual enlightenment are enabled to open the consciousness of those who seek them out. In reality, such a teacher does not impart truth at all, but, in much the same way as the sunlight opens the bud into the flower, he merely opens the closed door so that the truth already embodied within the consciousness of the student can flow forth into visible and tangible manifestation. This was the significance of the Master's words: "And I, if I be lifted up from the earth, will draw all men unto me." In proportion as he himself has received some measure of spiritual insight and realization, a teacher can draw others up to that level of consciousness.

The reason an individual becomes a student of spiritual truth in the first place, devoting his time and effort to studying and attending lectures and classes, is because something he has read or heard strikes a responsive chord, and inwardly he has a feeling that this is not something new, but is something he always has known. Many times students have remarked: "Deep down in my heart I have known this truth all my life, but I never was able to put it into words." No real and lasting benefit can be derived from this work except by those who feel an inner warmth and sensitivity, because such individuals are meeting their own state of consciousness face to face.

Truth is infinite, and truth is within you. Infinity cannot be confined to anything less than infinity. Therefore, your true nature is infinite, and it is from the depths of your being that all good must flow. This is the basis from which the message of The Infinite Way proceeds, and the purpose of its teaching is to enable you to open consciousness that you may become cognizant and aware of the truth that already is within you, and to enable you to bring that truth into expression and activity in your experience.

As spiritual understanding expands in consciousness, it becomes evident that desire, even every right and good desire, is an acknowledgment of lack, and that this is the error that is separating you from your good. Desire springs from the belief that our experience is lacking in some respects, and we believe that if only we can possess certain things or enjoy certain conditions, our lives will be more harmonious. But the truth is this: since the nature of your being is infinite, all that is necessary and needful for the fulfilment of your experience *already is established within you—here and now!* Nothing will be, or. can be, added to you. "Therefore I say unto you, What things soever ye desire, when ye pray, believe that ye receive them, and ye shall have them." In the sight of God, the only acceptable prayer is a silent communion with the gentle Presence that is within your own being—"Thank you, Father, *I am.*"

This realization of the kingdom of God within you is the birth of the Christ in consciousness, and with this revelation the search for God has ended, for how can you possibly search for that which you are? Can you search for integrity, honesty, fidelity? No, because you are well aware that these qualities are embodied within you, and are not to be found elsewhere. So it is with supply, health, companionship, love—these very things are embodied within you, and as you learn to commune with the Father, and rest in the understanding of your completeness, wholeness, and perfection, they begin to flow forth from you.

This state of spiritual completeness is not due to

any personal virtue or effort. Rather, it is a state of God being—the allness of the Godhead made manifest. The Master patiently and repeatedly taught that the indwelling Christ is that which heals, maintains, and sustains: "I can of mine own self do nothing. . . . I seek not mine own will, but the will of the Father which hath sent me. If I bear witness of myself, my witness is not true. . . . My doctrine is not mine, but his that sent me. . . . My Father worketh hitherto, and I work. . . . Believest thou not that I am in the Father, and the Father in me? the words that I speak unto you I speak not of myself: but the Father that dwelleth in me, he doeth the works. . . . Verily, verily, I say unto you, The Son can do nothing of himself, but what he seeth the Father do: for what things soever he doeth, these also doeth the Son likewise. . . . For as the Father hath life in himself; so hath he given to the Son to have life in himself." The power and authority of Jesus was the completeness of the Son of God, the Christ, made evident through Jesus.

God is the reality of your being, and Christ is your true identity. In God, in Christ, you are fulfilled; and to the extent of your realization of this truth you are enabled to draw upon your Christhood. By way of illustration, suppose you are confronted with what appears to be a great need. From the standpoint of humanhood, you have only a few visible loaves and fishes, and since you have no storehouses or reserves there is no apparent way to meet it. From the standpoint of your Christhood, however, you can bless that which you have, knowing that these are not limited, finite loaves and fishes:

these are God's supply, His own creation, and therefore they are *infinite*—and in that recognition of the infinite nature of your being, the need is met, for "the Father that dwelleth in me, he doeth the works."

"In the beginning was the Word, and the Word was with God, and the Word was God. The same was in the beginning with God. All things were made by him: and without him was not any thing made that was made. In him was life; and the life was the light of men." In the beginning was God, and God was Spirit, and everything that came forth came forth from Spirit. Everything is infinite—whether loaves and fishes, dollar bills, ideas, or words—the source is the same; the substance is the same. But it is extremely important not to place one thing or idea in the category of Spirit, and another in the category of matter, for in so doing the combination is broken.

You cannot add to a vessel already full, and so, from the basis that the infinite allness of God is embodied within you, you must make a transition of consciousness. Now that you are becoming aware of the infinity of your true nature, you must learn to draw back and abide in that infinity, so that the love, healing, supply, security, and companionship necessary for your development and fulfilment will flow forth from within. No longer will your prayer be a reaching out to God, nor will you ever again desire or seek any form of demonstration—except one, the demonstration of the presence of God. Jesus taught: "Ask, and it shall be given you; seek, and ye shall find; knock, and it shall be opened unto you." But he also taught that we should take no thought for our lives, and so we must be ever watchful of what we desire. Since God is Spirit, we do not ask God for material things. The desire that is prayer is for the realization of God, and so henceforth our desire must be for the gifts of the Spirit. "For every one that asketh receiveth; and he that seeketh findeth; and to him that knocketh it shall be opened."

Scripture tells us that we know not how to pray, nor what things to pray for, but that the Spirit Itself makes intercession for us. And so, when you pray, acknowledge that you know not what to pray for, and that all you are asking is for spiritual light. If, at this very moment, God could be so personalized as to be available right where you are, would it ever occur to you to ask or even think of anything of a material nature? Would you not know that in the intimacy of that divine association God would know your every need and provide it? Therefore, the only true prayer is for the realization of God—God omnipresent, omnipotent, omniscient. God is the life and fulfilment of all being, and you must realize that God *is* closer than breathing, and actually as tangible as though He were standing beside you. If you have God, must you ask for a home or employment? If you have God, must you ask for love, or health, or supply? All who have experienced God know, without doubt, that in His presence is fulness of life. Henceforth we will abstain from all prayer that might have as its object a person, place, thing, condition, or circumstance. Instead, our prayer will be an unceasing song of gratitude that God is love, the Father-Mother principle of our existence, the all-knowing mind; and we will live in the constant awareness that "the Lord thy God is with thee whithersoever thou goest."

True prayer is communion with God through frequent meditation, whereby the mind is stilled and receptive, the inner ear alert and attentive; in which, instead of mulling over our human thoughts, we await the divine thoughts that emanate from within. In this silence there is no mental exertion whatsoever—we realize: "Be still, and know that I am God." Remember this: no good can come to you; all good is to flow from you. See yourself as Self-complete in God, to such a degree that if you should happen to leave your home without a cent in your pocket, everything needful for the day's experience would be forthcoming; or, in the case of an emergency or disaster, from out of the depths of the infinite nature of your own Christhood, you would be maintained and sustained, and able to care for others.

It is in this way that the spiritual light which emanates and radiates from your being will become the guide for others who are as yet unaware of the kingdom of God within them. Not that you will give them of your light—oh, no! you will simply reveal the truth that is within them—that they too are Self-complete in God.

The Fifteenth Chapter of John

I am the true vine, and my Father is the husbandman. . . . Abide in me, and I in you. As the branch cannot bear fruit of itself, except it abide in the vine; no more can ye, except ye abide in me.

If you will take a few minutes to carefully observe a tree, you will better comprehend the profound meaning of these words of the Master. A tree is comprised of a root system, a trunk, from which spring the branches, and fruit. Picture yourself as a branch that is being nourished and sustained through the trunk, which draws its life sustenance from the earth in which the tree is rooted and grounded. Are you, as a branch, dependent upon any other branch? No, the branch is one with the trunk. You, the visible branch, are connected and at-one with the vine, the invisible Christ of your being, and this spiritual relationship is the connecting link with the Father. God is the infinite creative principle of the universe, in which your real being is founded and established, and the allness of the Godhead flows through the invisible Christhood into visible expression as fruitage in the way of health, supply, home, love, and all the things needful for the fulfilment of your experience.

Most of the world can acknowledge itself as the visible branch, but it cannot concede the invisible, and by far the greater part, the vine, because the vine is not physical—it is spiritual, the very animating and motivating principle of all life. If one were to dissect a seed in the endeavor to find life, one would fail: the seed is embodied in life, and life flows in and out, around, about and through the seed, causing it to break open, root, sprout, take form and appear above the earth—but always the life is invisible. Each individual has within himself this same invisible life force or power, the Christ, through which he is rooted and grounded in the infinite universal Life. As we come into an understanding of this principle, the words of the Master become alive with meaning, and we comprehend that when he said: "Take no thought for your life . . . for it is the Father's good pleasure to give you the kingdom," he was telling us that all our good must flow out from the Spirit of God which abides within us. We can readily see that the branch cannot bear fruit except it abide in the vine, but as we do abide in the vine, we can drop all concern.

If you can accept the fact that the visible part of your being is connected with the invisible Christ, which is completely at-one with the Father, will you ever again take anxious thought? Is it not true that every fearful and doubting thought has been based upon the belief that this visible, finite, and material form constituted our being? What is this but a sense of separation from God? On the other hand, can you imagine anyone who is living in the conscious realization of his oneness with God ever fearing or worrying about his well-being? In the absence of this realization, it is only natural for one who considers himself a human being, separate and apart from God, to fear. As you consciously and inwardly become aware that you, as a branch, are connected with the invisible vine, which, in its turn, is at-one with the Father, and that all the Father hath is flowing to you through the vine, will you any longer be concerned with fruitage? No! You will merely stand still and rest, and let the fruitage appear. And you may be assured that *the fruitage will appear*, simply because of this contact. Of ourselves, we can do nothing, but from the Father to the Christ, and from the Christ to the Son, flows the infinity of good. Our oneness with God, having been established in the beginning, is now consciously realized.

Heretofore, we have thought of ourselves as individuals who must pray to a God in heaven in order to receive our good, but now our eyes are opened, and we see that our good must be permitted to flow from the infinity of our being; and that we ourselves must open out a way for it to escape in order that it may appear in visible form. The tree is complete because of its contact with the universal life principle—which principle automatically acts as a catalysis whereby the essences of the sun, air, water, and substances of the earth are distributed through the tree, providing it with all the elements necessary to produce abundant fruitage. As long as the tree remains firmly rooted in the ground, it is a complete unit; but separate and apart from the ground it will shortly wither and die. One with the Father, you are a complete unit—infinitely complete, possessing all the essence and substance, qualities and attributes of the Father—love, life, law, truth, mind, Spirit, Soul. You are Self-complete, sustained, maintained, and fulfilled through your conscious oneness with God.

It is up to you, individually, to so assimilate a comprehensive knowledge and understanding of the letter of truth that you can come into some degree of this realization of oneness, in order that you may permit the truth to flow in greater and ever-increasing measure. It is necessary to eat and drink of this truth, to digest it, and make it a part of your very being; and although it may seem four months to the harvest, there will come that day when "the fields are white already to harvest," and you will begin to see the outpouring of it. Gradually, you will become aware of the establishment of an unusual inner peace, and little by little, as fears and doubts drop away, you lose concern for tomorrow. And when, ultimately, you realize that you do not live by bread alone, but by the Word that proceedeth out of the mouth of God, your salvation is complete and your demonstration is made unto eternity, for then you will know that this truth is the substance of your being—it is your manna, water, bread, supply, protection, safety, security—and never again will you permit thought to go outside your own being in the desire for attainment of any person or any thing. Instead of thinking in terms of the outer material realm, you will be thinking in terms of your inner contact with the Spirit, from which will pour life eternal in ever abundant measure.

Spiritual Power

The Infinite Way is a revelation of the spiritual power inherent in all men. This power is realized only in proportion as material and mental force is relinquished—and silence is attained.

In the silence, a voice is heard, a vision is seen, a presence is felt. We are now contemplating the Unknown.

Preparation for this experience has been the many years of study, meditation, and practice of spiritual truth; and through association with the seers and sages of all ages by pondering their inspired spiritual revelations. Over these years, interest in oneself has lessened until the problems of human existence are no longer a personal concern—rather, they are seen objectively and handled as world beliefs. Thus one also loses the sense of personal pleasure, and in its place an inner joy arises and engulfs one. This joy is never dependent on outer stimulation. It is a constant, flowing state of harmonious being, which is not interrupted even during temporary illness, lack, or other discord.

In this state of harmonious being, nothing that transpires in the outer realm is construed as failure; but rather, as an incentive for deeper and more constant study and meditation. Nor is it possible to feel success, since this is realized as an activity of the Spirit and not of oneself. This is the true detachment.

Never is spiritual power *used* to attain any end. Without conscious effort, it is that which is always expressing itself as the activity of individual being; and, knowing our need even before we do, it likewise supplies and fulfills without our "taking thought".

Once realized, spiritual power takes over the responsibility, direction, and action of our lives, and the harmonious functioning of our bodies. It draws to us all those necessary for the fulfilment of our experience, and everything needful for joyous living. Even in the midst of active family, business, or professional interests, the quiet of the contemplative life is now assured. This also is the true detachment. The weight of personal responsibility has lifted, and God now bears us on Its wings, and covers us with Its feathers. The experience of living beside the still waters and in green pastures becomes a living reality.

*　　　*　　　*

While browsing in a second-hand book store, one of our students found the following verse inscribed on the fly-leaf of an old worn copy of the *Bhagavad-Gita*. This poem, which is attributed to Paul Oregan, aptly presents the principle of oneness with God:

Let what will come! Old faiths be overthrown
And new beliefs give old beliefs the lie:
One thing I hold mid crash of creed and throne
Forever I am I.

Before time was, or thought of day or night,
Before God woke the silence with Its voice,
I, hidden in the Being Infinite
In silence did rejoice.

And I, the pilgrim of eternity,
Can laugh to see eternities roll on;
For though God say: There shall be naught but me;
Yet, He and I are One.

CHAPTER ELEVEN

SCRIPTURAL PRINCIPLES

MANY of the ageless truths and principles which constitute the foundation upon which the structure of The Infinite Way is built are to be found in the Old as well as the New Testament. "Hear, O Israel: the Lord our God is one Lord. . . . Ye shall not need to fight in this battle: set yourselves, stand ye still, and see the salvation of the Lord with you. . . . Be strong and courageous, be not afraid nor dismayed for the king of Assyria, nor for all the multitude that is with him. . . . With him is an arm of flesh; but with us is the Lord our God to help us, and to fight our battles. . . . Fear not: for I have redeemed thee, I have called thee by thy name: thou art mine. . . . Thou wilt keep him in perfect peace, whose mind is stayed on thee: because he trusteth in thee."

The Psalmist's spiritual perception and awareness were especially keen and comprehensive, and his songs of praise and thanksgiving confidently bear witness to the realization of God's presence. Probably the greatest and most assuring truths to be found in all scripture are the simple, yet profound, statements: "The Lord is my shepherd; I shall not want," and "He that dwelleth in the secret place of the most High shall abide under the shadow of the Almighty." Many other of the Psalms set forth the promises of grace to be enjoyed by those who place their confidence and trust in God. The 146th Psalm, for instance, is one such example:

Praise ye the Lord. Praise the Lord, O my soul. While I live will I praise the Lord: I will sing praises unto my God while I have any being.

Put not your trust in princes, nor in the son of man, in whom there is no help. His breath goeth forth, he returneth to his earth; in that very day his thoughts perish.

Happy is he that hath the God of Jacob for his help, whose hope is in the Lord his God: Which made heaven, and earth, the sea, and all that therein is: which keepeth truth for ever:

Which executeth judgment for the oppressed: which giveth food to the hungry. The Lord looseth the prisoners: The Lord openeth the eyes of the blind: the Lord raiseth them that are bowed down: the Lord loveth the righteous: The Lord preserveth the strangers; he relieveth the fatherless and widow: but the way of the wicked he turneth upside down.

The Lord shall reign for ever, even thy God, O Zion, unto all generations. Praise ye the Lord.

The world has made the grave mistake of believing that there is a mighty God in heaven who, eventually, is going to do all these wonderful things of which this Psalm speaks, and so, thinking it has no further responsibility, it sits back and waits for something to happen. But that is not the way. The Master taught: "God is a Spirit: and they that worship him must worship him in spirit and in truth."

To make such truths active in our experience, we must make contact with the Spirit of God that is within us, and if we do *not* make and maintain this inner contact through constant prayer and receptivity, we soon find that God is not doing much in our experience.

The pressure of the world, with its false idea of "divide and conquer" has made us natural enemies, and it would separate us, not only from God but from each other—employers from employees, buyers from sellers, capital from labor, man from wife, parent from child. But the fundamental teaching of the Master's message is oneness—at-one-ment with God—whereby he taught: "I and my Father are one"; and that because of this state of spiritual oneness, it is not necessary to take thought for our lives. His life was a perfect example of what Paul refers to as "prayer without ceasing"—always he maintained a state of conscious oneness in union with God, because he was well aware of the fact that he had nothing to offer in the way of healing or teaching except as the Spirit of God was made an active and conscious part of his being, and permitted to dwell within him. Only because of this conscious at-one-ment with God was Jesus able to say: "I have meat to eat that ye know not of," and later, ". . . whosoever drinketh of the water that I shall give him shall never thirst; but the water . . . shall be in him a well of water springing up into everlasting life."

Each student of The Infinite Way must learn to apply this principle in his daily life. But, you say, "I am one individual among billions, and I am no longer young—how am I to earn a living and enjoy any degree of security and satisfaction unless I, too, enter the struggle of competition and contention? How can I receive this truth which will forever release me from the laws and beliefs and discords of the world?" There is one way, and only one way, to receive this truth, and that is by establishing, as a constant and continuing activity of your own consciousness, the realization that you are one with God, the source of all good. Every day, without fail, you must meditate upon this principle of oneness— realizing that because you are one with God, you are one with every individual, with all being; that you are at-one with all forms of good—activity, employment, service, supply, companionship, joy, peace, and prosperity; and that all that is necessary to unfold and reveal your demonstration of harmony is forever flowing from the divine Source within your own being. It is true, of course, that as a person you *are* alone and lost, but in attaining conscious union with God, the fulness of the Godhead is forever protecting, providing, and caring for your every need.

Mankind's greatest tragedy is that of seeking supply, safety, security, and peace from men and nations, because physical union and material might do not constitute strength. Never, never seek your good from the world, because in so doing you miss the way. *Seek only the realization of God!* Seek only the conscious realization of your oneness with the Source of all good, and then become a beholder as this invisible spiritual power draws unto you all the things necessary for your fulfilment. The passage, "Put not your trust in princes, nor in the son of man, in whom there is no help," is a reminder that all too often we place our reliance on man—on government, on customer, husband, wife, student, practitioner, instead of the Lord "which keepeth truth for ever." As we learn to rely on God, the activity of truth in our consciousness re-establishes us, and becomes the law unto our experience. Without this activity of truth we are victims of all the physical, material, and mental laws of world belief, but when we are aware that ". . . greater is he that is in you, than he that is in the world," the dominion of God is manifest in our experience. Indeed, "Happy is he that hath the God of Jacob for his help, whose hope is in the Lord his God."

The 147th Psalm

Praise ye the Lord: for it is good to sing praises unto our God; for it is pleasant; and praise is comely.

The Lord doth build up Jerusalem: he gathereth together the outcasts of Israel. He healeth the broken in heart, and bindeth up their wounds. He telleth the number of the stars; he calleth them all by their names.

Great is our Lord, and of great power: his understanding is infinite. The Lord lifteth up the meek: he casteth the wicked down to the ground.

Sing unto the Lord with thanksgiving; sing praise upon the harp unto our God: Who covereth the heaven with clouds, who prepareth rain for the earth, who maketh grass to grow upon the mountains. He giveth to the beast his food, and to the young ravens which cry.

He delighteth not in the strength of the horse: he taketh not pleasure in the legs of a man. The Lord taketh pleasure in them that fear him, in those that hope in his mercy.

Praise the Lord, O Jerusalem; praise thy God, O Zion. For he hath strengthened the bars of thy gates; he hath blessed thy children within thee. He maketh peace in thy borders, and filleth thee with the finest of the wheat. He sendeth forth his commandment upon earth: his word runneth very swiftly.

He giveth snow like wool: he scattereth the hoarfrost like ashes. He casteth forth his ice like morsels: who can stand before his cold?

He sendeth out his word, and melteth them: he causeth his wind to blow, and the waters flow.

He sheweth his word unto Jacob, his statutes and his judgments unto Israel. He hath not dealt so with any nation: and as for his judgments, they have not known them. Praise ye the Lord.

Another of the great scriptural truths is to be found in this Psalm. As students, we give much thought to "our" understanding, many times lamenting our inadequacies: "Oh, if I just had more understanding perhaps I could heal this, or accomplish that." But here we learn: "Great is our Lord, and of great power: *his understanding is infinite.*" Therefore, our understanding is of no importance—it is *His understanding* that does the works, and *our only part and requirement is to turn within and receive His understanding.* The truth we know merely represents our understanding or knowledge at this present level of consciousness, and if we depend solely upon that we will, eventually, come to the end of that understanding. We must learn to turn to God and let His understanding flow from within, for there, there is no limit and no end—His understanding is infinite—and therein lies our salvation.

We will suppose that a problem is presented to you. You have given up the old concept of petitionary prayer, you have relinquished the old idea of affirmation and denial, and, following the Middle Path, you see it as neither good nor evil—but, nevertheless, you are faced with a pressing situation, and so you ask: "How do I apply this truth? How can I avail myself of God's understanding?" In answer, we will again take a principle from the Master, one in which a law of tremendous depth is revealed: "For unto every one that hath shall be given; and he shall have abundance: but from him that hath not shall be taken away even that which he hath." If you are to say, "Oh, but I haven't sufficient understanding with which to meet this claim—I haven't studied long enough—I don't know how to go about it," you have done all that is necessary to impoverish yourself. You have declared your own lack, that you *have not*, and that is what you will demonstrate—perfect and complete lack. Only in the degree that you believe fulfilment, can fulfilment be achieved and demonstrated. Acknowledge that you have not, and you will demonstrate have not. Acknowledge that you have, and you will demonstrate have. So remember this principle: "For unto every one that hath shall be given, and he shall have abundance."

Surely every student knows at least one statement of truth which, to him, holds some particular significance. All right then, you *have* that one statement, and so you acknowledge, not that you lack, but that you *have*! Now, as you open consciousness in the silence, pondering that one statement, another will come to mind, and another, and soon you will discover that this is not the truth that *you* know—*this is the truth that God knows!*

We are not at all concerned with your understanding or mine—the important thing is: How much understanding has God, and have we access to that understanding? If we have, what you or I know is of no consequence. It is not necessary to search your memory for some spiritual or metaphysical statement of affirmation or denial with which to meet this claim; and, even if you do, chances are you will come up with something that is of no value in meeting the problem. You have only to turn within, in acknowledgment of the fulness of God's presence, and you will find His Word to be quick and sharp and powerful. Many times our demonstration of harmony is blocked by claiming lack and insufficiency under a cloak of false humility by saying: "I don't know very much truth." It really makes no difference how much or how little truth you know—it is the *Word of God* that meets our needs, and *His understanding is infinite!*

The Psalm continues: "The Lord lifteth up the meek: . . . He delighteth not in the strength of the horse: he taketh not pleasure in the legs of a man. The Lord taketh pleasure in them that fear him, in those that hope in his mercy." Here the claim of material might and physical power is set aside. Heretofore we have believed we were bringing forth the physical strength of our human bodies and the intelligence of our human minds: whereas, if we were to reverse that and realize that all strength and wisdom is of God and is, therefore, spiritual, we would be capable of bringing forth infinitely more in the way of bodily perfection and mental ability. God is the substance and law of your body, the intelligence of your mind, the abundance of your supply, the nature of your being: and just as you can call upon Him for statements of truth, or for carrying out your activities, so also can you call upon Him for the health of your body and mind, and all the blessings of harmonious living. "He sendeth forth his commandment upon earth: his word runneth swiftly. . . . He sheweth his word unto Jacob, his statutes and his judgments unto Israel." He sheweth His Word unto all who are willing to turn within, in conscious union with God, that His understanding, His strength, His wisdom may be shown forth.

Again and again I must repeat: this truth must be active in your consciousness in order to make it available in your experience. Merely to say: "I and my Father are one," and "To him that hath shall be given," is meaningless repetition, unless you yourself declare these words with conviction and act upon them—draw upon the truth you already have and the truth will flow; draw upon that dollar you already have and let the next one flow; draw upon that hour of service you already have and let the next hour flow—on unto eternity from the infinite Source within your own being.

239

God is our refuge and strength, a very present help in trouble.

Therefore will not we fear, though the earth be removed, and though the mountains be carried into the midst of the sea; Though the waters thereof roar and be troubled, though the mountains shake with the swelling thereof.

There is a river, the streams whereof shall make glad the city of God, the holy place of the tabernacles of the most High. God is in the midst of her; she shall not be moved: God shall help her, and that right early.

The heathen raged, the kingdoms were moved: he uttered his voice, the earth melted. The Lord of hosts is with us; the God of Jacob is our refuge.

Come, behold the works of the Lord, what desolations he hath made in the earth. He maketh wars to cease unto the end of the earth, he breaketh the bow, and cutteth the spear in sunder; he burneth the chariot in the fire.

Be still, and know that I am God: I will be exalted among the heathen, I will be exalted in the earth. The Lord of hosts is with us; the God of Jacob is our refuge.

•

It is absolutely true, of course, that God fills all space—God is here where we are, but He is also on the battlefield, in the hospitals, the prisons, the asylums; but that fact is of benefit to no one except those who have the realization of His presence. If we may be permitted to paraphrase the opening line of this Psalm, it should read: "The realization of God, the attainment and demonstration of God, is our refuge, a very present help in trouble"—and therefore, as we *dwell* in this consciousness we need have no fear, for regardless of their nature, the problems immediately confronting us will be solved.

There is a river, a river of life, a stream of God within each and every individual, awaiting recognition—and it is attained in the silence. If myriad unrelated thoughts race and tumble through your mind, pay no heed: that will not prevent God realization. The only thing that *can* prevent it is your unwillingness to set aside sufficient periods during the day for moments of receptive listening. As He utters His voice, the kingdoms of earth are moved. When, in meditation, you receive the divine impulse by the release of a deep, escaping breath, the still, small voice is announcing the presence and power of God within you, and you can be assured that the errors of sin, disease, lack, limitation, and death are melting away.

"Be still, and know that I am God." Always, God is uttering His voice within us, but much of the time we are not attuned and attentive. We must hear Him, become aware of Him, feel and recognize His presence in order to benefit. Much patience and constancy of endeavor must be devoted to these periods of quiet listening until such time as we are devoid of all human desires. Then, as He utters His voice within us, we become the instruments through which the bow, the spear, and the chariot of material sense and discord are made desolate. In time, the troubles of the nations of the world will disappear, not by praying to God, but by the realization of the omnipresence of divine love.

Love

The beloved disciple, John, tells us: "God is love; and he that dwelleth in love dwelleth in God, and God in him. . . . There is no fear in love; but perfect love casteth out fear." Paul says: "Love worketh no ill to his neighbor: therefore love is the fulfilling of the law." The love of which these great men write is divine, spiritual love, and to those of us on the spiritual path of life, it is important and imperative that our daily experience exemplify this love which fulfils the law.

In this year of 1956, the world is deeply entrenched in hatreds and animosities—racial, religious, ideological, and national. Is it possible that these intense hatreds, instigated by the struggle for power, will lead to world peace and harmony? The answer, obviously, is No!

There *is* a way to peace, however, and it is the way of love. And it is the true seekers after God who will be instrumental in bringing peace on earth, because the love of God and the peace that passeth understanding dwells in their hearts. Wherever there is love there, also, is peace and harmony. In the degree, therefore, that we, as students of The Infinite Way, consciously entertain spiritual peace and love within us, do we bring these to fruition on earth. Divine love is expressed wherever two or more are together, seeking nothing of each other, but ever joyous in any opportunity to serve and assist. This love is expressed and experienced in such simple things as a cheery "Aloha" greeting on meeting and parting, and in our courtesy and thoughtfulness and consideration for those for whom, and with whom, we work and associate.

All of God's love is available to us, and in the face of this fact it is strange and sad to contemplate how small is man's capacity for receiving it. The reason is that we seek love from each other, instead of from God. Although there is a measure of human love for family, community, and nation, this love will not solve the problems of the world, simply because all too often greater problems are created due to the degree of selfishness that enters into human emotions. Only as we can release each other from the bondage of duty, obligation, and debt, and dwell in the realization that *God alone is love*; that all love is of *God*; that our expectancy is of *God*; and that *God's love* fulfills the law—does love flow freely to us and, through us, to others.

The intense seeking for self is the reason for national and international discord, as well as individual. This exaggerated and insatiable sense of self-love, self-fear, self-ambition, self-greed—all and anything for self—is but ignorance of the truth. Whereas, "to know the Truth" is to know that our true Self is God, and includes within Itself all good—everything necessary for our unfoldment. To seek supply and safety and security at the expense of others, or to hope for peace and prosperity through war with others is folly. But to pray that all men everywhere, friend and foe alike, may know the infinite abundance of God's grace and the blessing of His presence is to receive God in the flesh—in harmony, health, joy, and abundance.

The way to demonstrate this life of love is to understand what makes some men selfish, sinful, evil, corrupt, and dangerous. Is it not easy to forgive when we realize that men's evils are not really evils—but ignorance of their true identity as the Christ-Self, the Son of God? Is it not easy to free others from duty or obligation when we realize that *we need nothing from another because our good already is within our own being*? "Forgive us our debts as *we* forgive our debtors; forgive us our trespasses as *we* forgive those who trespass against us" is no idle prayer. The Master's admonition to pray for our enemies and for those who persecute us are not lightly spoken words—these constitute the Word of God.

The evils that torture and torment the world do not come nigh the dwelling place of those who abide in love, who have released all men from obligation and debt, and who seek their good only in God. Spiritual love finds outlet through the pure in heart —those who have learned that God alone is supply; that God alone is their fortress and high tower; their husband, wife, or companion. Life lived in the spirit of sharing, co-operating, giving, serving, while at the same time expecting no human return, is the atmosphere into which God pours Itself liberally.

To the human being, intent solely upon self-preservation, self-ambition, self-gratification, this will seem a difficult way of life; and to him, it *is* difficult, if not almost impossible. To the truth student who has witnessed man's failure to solve the individual, national, and international problems, this Way of Love holds out a promise. To those who, through study, meditation, and devotion to a spiritual cause, have been touched by the Spirit of God, love is The Infinite Way of harmonious life; it is the fulfilling of the law. When divine love is our way of life, we no longer seek our good from each other, nor do we expect safety from a bomb-proof shelter, nor security from H-bombs, nor supply from doles, nor do we look to "man whose breath is in his nostrils" for reward, recognition, or gratitude. But, as we dwell in the realization of the omnipresence of God as "our shepherd," we experience every form of good in infinite measure.

The spiritual life is a state of grace, in which there is no need to take thought for our lives, what we shall eat or drink. Divine grace is our shield and buckler, our table in the wilderness. Here no thought of getting, acquiring, achieving enters in; but, rather, we experience God's infinite wisdom and power, the omnipresence even of those human and material things necessary to a joyous and harmonious life. "Your Father *knoweth* that ye have need of these things . . . for it is your Father's good pleasure to *give* you the kingdom."

Few people realize that in metaphysics, health is not so much a matter of receiving "treatments" as in *living the life of love*; thereby letting His peace flow to us and through us by forgiving and praying for those who despitefully use us; in giving of our substance, our service, our selves—with no expectancy of return or acknowledgment. Few students actually realize to what extent they are perpetuating

245

the discords of their experience by not yielding to this spiritual impulse of giving, forgiving, sharing, serving. It is only as we cast our bread of love upon the waters of our daily lives that it returns to us—full, complete, and perfect.

A Prayer

O Divine Master, grant that I may not so much seek to be consoled as to console; to be understood as to understand; to be loved as to love; for it is in giving that we receive, it is in pardoning that we are pardoned, and it is in dying that we are born to eternal life.

St. Francis of Assisi

To hold no one in bondage to his errors, sins, debts, or obligations, is to find release from these for oneself. This is to know love—and love is life eternal.

Through my realization of God, I have learned this momentous lesson: when the spirit of love touches us, we are instantly freed from death—for love, it is revealed, is life. When love fills our consciousness there is no hate, no fear, no sin, and, therefore, no death. Eternal life is achieved through love here on earth, and the passing from human sight is now an advancing state of consciousness from one plane of life to another. There comes a moment's intuitive flash when the realization dawns that death can no longer occur, that release from the need of death has been given. I have been given eternal life on earth with the full knowledge that when I pass from human sight, my going will be a progressive step in the Path of Light. This living in love dissolves the false sense of self, and reveals our true Self—infinite, perfect, and immortal.

Spiritual Attainment

In the course of a purely human existence, we eat but are not really fed, we drink but our thirst is not quenched. We earn wages, but they bring little in the way of lasting satisfaction. Certainly it is right and good that we eat and drink and earn wages, but as we do these things to the glory of God, by realizing God as the substance and activity of our lives and being, we find that it takes much less to satisfy, and yet, our every need is met. As we continue to eat and drink and earn wages, let us put forth all effort in the name of the Lord. With all sustenance, with all activities, with all pleasures and joys, recognize God as the substance and source. With all earnings, recognize God as that which supplies, bestows, blesses, and multiplies, and watch the infinite nature of your good unfold. Spiritual living is not the suspension of the natural and normal activities and pleasures of our experience. On the contrary, as we approach life from the standpoint of God, an entirely new concept of love, of sharing, of being, enters into our daily experiences, and we find each day glorified and blessed with new joys, new prosperity, new fulfilments.

"I have meat to eat that ye know not of"—this meat of which Jesus spoke is the understanding of God as the law and activity, the source and substance of all good.

Across the Desk

Until the practice of the presence of God in our daily and hourly experience is brought about through our conscious effort, we can hardly be prepared for the deeper things that are brought out in meditation and in communion with God. The fact that you are devoting your time and effort to the study of spiritual truth is proof that your desire is not merely for more human good, but for an actual spiritual way of life, and a knowledge of the deeper secrets and mysteries of spiritual consciousness.

The latest books in our growing family of Infinite Way writings, *Practicing the Presence*[1] and *The Art of Meditation*,[2] have set the stage for the immediate practice of meditation, contemplation, cogitation—leading to communion and, of course, finally, to that last step in our experience—conscious union with God. Those of you who are numbered as our very earnest students must take these books for deep and serious study, and put their teachings into actual daily practice. These new books, together with our main textbook, *The Infinite Way*,[3] will bring a greater depth of meditation than you have ever experienced.

Surely you must understand that it is impossible for me to carry you to the place of realization unless you co-operate with this intensity of study. I could not write this to the world—for the world is interested primarily in those things that will give it

[1] By Joel S. Goldsmith (London: L. N. Fowler & Co. Ltd., 1956).

[2] By Joel S. Goldsmith (New York: Harper & Brothers Publishers, 1956).

[3] By Joel S. Goldsmith, *op. cit.*

ease in its material affairs, greater comfort and profit, or greater health and human good. Little does it care whether it gains its good through God, through pills or dollar bills, just as long as it gets a greater measure of human happiness and satisfaction. Certainly this cannot be true of our Infinite Way students, but I well know that as our consciousness becomes more deeply imbued with the things and the knowledge and the awareness of the Spirit, our outer circumstances improve, and we go into the realization of health and supply, peace among our friends and neighbors, and, ultimately, into international good will. Few have had more proof than I that the harmonies of this world appear in proportion to the depth of our spiritual vision. Certainly those of you who know me are aware of the great joys and blessings that have come into my experience through my conscious communion with God, and through the experience of union with God with which I have been blessed.

Those of you who meet me in my travels in all the countries around the globe know that my life is a continuous round of joy and bliss, of harmony, and peace on earth. Many of you have witnessed, not only the love I have for the men and women and children of this world, but the love that is extended to me and to this activity of The Infinite Way. I can assure you that the fruitage of our spiritual vision is great, but it is not upon this fruitage that I should like to dwell, but upon the experience, itself, of contact with God, and of ultimate union with God. Here, truly, we find our Self-completeness in Him, and all perfection manifested in infinite abundance.

It is also true, as many of you know, that at times inharmonies and discords have entered my human experience, but perhaps you do not realize that all of these experiences were instrumental in bringing me nearer to God, and closer to this ultimate joy and spiritual bliss which you witness interpreted in terms of human good. Not for one single moment would I miss the deep valley experiences that have come into my life, for I can assure you that my mountain-top experiences are proportionate to those valley depths. Not only that, but one descent into a valley has resulted in the ascension of many mountain tops. Since the message of The Infinite Way is purely an individual experience, and is a spiritual one, I rarely refer to myself or to my personal life. But I do so at this time that you may never forget that the few, the very few, inharmonies and discords that have come into my experience are not to be regretted, nor are they to be thought of as failures to achieve the spiritual life. On the contrary, often they have been the means of great spiritual victories.

Well do I know the troubles, the trials, and tribulations that many of you have experienced and, perhaps, are experiencing even now. Indeed I do because I, too, have known from actual experience serious illness of body, periods of financial distress, and failures in human relationships. But each of these trials has contributed to the entire message of The Infinite Way, and to the health and sufficiency and abundance of God, and the joys of my relationships. I am able to bear witness to you and to this message and, of course, I can also glory in that my own experiences have contributed to the spiritual good now coming into the lives of many of you. From all over the world my mail, which has assumed proportions beyond belief, is filled with glowing messages of harmonies that have come into the lives of those who have received the message of The Infinite Way. None of this could be, dear friends, but for the degree of study and devotion that you bring to this message.

CHAPTER TWELVE

THE CHRIST

Believest thou not that I am in the Father, and the Father in me? the words that I speak unto you I speak not of myself: but the Father that dwelleth in me, he doeth the works.

Believe me that I am in the Father, and the Father in me: or else believe me for the very works' sake.

Verily, verily, I say unto you, He that believeth on me, the works that I do shall he do also; and greater works than these shall he do; because I go unto my Father.

And whatsoever ye shall ask in my name, that will I do, that the Father may be glorified in the Son.

If ye shall ask any thing in my name, I will do it.

If ye love me, keep my commandments.

And I will pray the Father, and he shall give you another Comforter, that he may abide with you for ever;

Even the Spirit of truth; whom the world cannot receive, because it seeth him not, neither knoweth him: but ye know him; for he dwelleth with you, and shall be in you.

I will not leave you comfortless: I will come to you.

Yet a little while, and the world seeth me no more; but ye see me: because I live, ye shall live also.

John 14:10-19

IN order to reach the kingdom of heaven, we must transcend the realm of mind and thought to the heights where the realm of Spirit unfolds and discloses itself. Upon entering the kingdom, we receive, within ourselves, the Word of God; the light of the Christ; the Spirit of God in man. Although we strive and press onward toward the kingdom only that the Word be received—always the Word is made flesh and dwells among us. Every time It is heard, It becomes manifest in the outer realm. Every time the divine impulse is felt, it becomes visible and tangible without. This Word of God is the substance of all form, the substance of all demonstration, the bread of life, the water of life eternal, the wine of inspiration; and therefore, when faced with any appearance of discord, inwardly we can say: "I and my Father are one. . . . All that the Father hath is mine. . . . I have meat to eat the world knoweth not of."

The Word of God is the activity of the Christ in individual consciousness. Christ is the secret of harmonious, joyous, peaceful, and fruitful living: but each must find for himself the way to contact It, to hear It, and to realize It. The Christ cannot be attained by suggestion, nor given by another, but only by the actual realization within the consciousness of the individual. This is not an easy matter of accomplishment, because of the countless generations through which we have lived in a sense of separation from God; but it is a task to which we must dedicate ourselves, through prayer, contemplation, meditation, and communion, until we actually realize the presence of the indwelling Christ. After that realization, we eagerly surrender our sense of humanhood, and become a beholder as Christ lives our lives; and regardless of what outer phase or condition we may be presenting to the world, inwardly we are remembering: "Thou wilt never leave me, nor forsake me. . . . Thou, in the midst of me, art mighty. . . . I do not live by bread alone, but by every Word that proceedeth out of the mouth of God. . . . Thy Word within me is life eternal."

"Believest thou not that I am in the Father, and the Father in me?" This is a universal truth: you are in the Father and the Father is in you. The Word of God in the midst of you is the mighty power and the presence of all good. "Abide in me, and I in you. As the branch cannot bear fruit of itself, except it abide in the vine; no more can ye, except ye abide in me. . . . He that abideth in me, and I in him, the same bringeth forth much fruit: for without me ye can do nothing. . . . If ye abide in me, and my words abide in you, ye shall ask what ye will, and it shall be done unto you. . . . As the Father hath loved me, so have I loved you: continue ye in my love. These things have I spoken unto you, that my joy might remain in you, and that your joy may be full."

The dictionary defines the word "abide" as: to stay; to continue in a place; to dwell, sojourn; to remain stable or fixed in some state; to continue; to await expectantly. This is exactly what we must practice from morning until night—"Abide in me, and I in you. As the branch cannot bear fruit of itself, except it abide in the vine: no more can ye, except ye abide in me . . . for without me you can do nothing." Your humanhood is not equal to survive the ups and downs, the trials and tribulations of this world—of yourself you can do nothing. The Master was well aware of this truth, but he also knew that because the branch is one with the vine, the fulness of the Godhead is forever flowing through it.

In this understanding, meditation and communion no longer consist of words and thoughts, declarations and denials, but are now an attitude of intent and quiet listening, of expectancy, and confidence that the Father's desire is pure. God has no object except to reveal Himself to you, so "Be still, and know that I am God"—be still, that the Word may impart and reveal Itself within you—*in full confidence that It will reveal Itself*. And so, as you sit in the silence, remember that you are reaching deep down within the center of your own being to that invisible vine, the Christ, wherein is the meat, the wine, the water, and the bread of life, sustaining you unto all eternity.

Paul's immortal and enduring words: "I can do all things through Christ which strengtheneth me," are a promise and a guide to all who would abide in the truth. This does not mean that your meditation periods are spent acquainting the Christ with your problems and needs, but by confidently *knowing* that you can do all things through the realization of His presence. Suddenly, the inner impulse comes to you and announces the presence of the peaceful, yet all-powerful, Christ. It may speak in words or a vision; you may be conscious of an assurance of peace and rest; or you may feel an actual sense of release as if the weight of the world had been lifted from your shoulders. In some way, the Christ makes evident Its presence—"I am with you alway, even unto the end of the world. I am the way, the truth, and the life. Did I not promise I would send a Comforter in my name, that he may abide with you forever?" This assurance is the Christ at the center of your being, which strengthens you. Of mine own self, I can do nothing, *but I can do all things through Christ*—Christ, which comforts, redeems, upholds, maintains, sustains, enlightens, and guides me. I can do all things, regardless of the demand, for I have the Christ, "even the Spirit of truth, whom the world cannot receive, because it seeth him not, neither knoweth him."

In the silence we open ourselves "That he would grant you, according to the riches of his glory, to be strengthened with might by his Spirit in the inner man." It is in the inner man that we must receive His Spirit. It is in the inner man that we must be strengthened, and as we are so strengthened His Word appears as bodily and mental completeness and perfection, and as all that is necessary for the maintenance and sustenance of the outer man.

"Believest thou not that I am in the Father, and the Father in me? . . . Believe me that I am in the Father, and the Father in me: or else believe me for the very works' sake."

Faith is not an understanding of the mind, not an acquired knowledge of truth, not a blind belief, not an ignorant superstition. Faith is an inner, spiritual discernment whereby we behold the Christ and feel, inwardly, that which the world knows not. Spiritual discernment is the ability to see that which is invisible, to hear that which is inaudible, and to know that which is unknowable. The English poet-mystic, Francis Thompson, expresses this truth in the following lines:

> O world invisible, we view thee,
> O world intangible, we touch thee,
> O world unknowable, we know thee,
> Inapprehensible, we clutch thee![1]

With that understanding we have *faith*, and only then can we behold the Christ. You will remember that although Jesus had healed and fed and taught multitudes of people throughout his ministry, only five hundred beheld the risen Christ—and that was by an inner knowing, an inner recognition, an inner vision of grace. Even "faith as a grain of mustard seed" is sufficient to move mountains. That faith is attained by being rooted and grounded in love—love for God, love for your neighbor, and love for the indwelling Christ.

The Master gave us two great commandments: first, "Thou shalt love the Lord thy God with all thy heart, and with all thy soul, and with all thy mind"; and second, "Thou shalt love thy neighbor as thyself." And, furthermore, he said: "On these two commandments hang all the law and the

---

[1] *In No Strange Land.*

prophets." To hate, to fear, or to place power in anything that has form is an act of idolatry; but when we love God with all our heart, and with all our soul, and with all our mind, *that love is a realization of God as the all and only power*. To love our neighbor as ourself begins on the spiritual level. It means that we are not to bear false witness against our neighbor —we are not to call our friend good nor our enemy evil, but spiritual. We must rise above all appearances of good and evil, and know our neighbor as the Son of God.

We know God as Spirit, love, life, truth— wholeness, completeness, perfection; and so, seeing things as they *are*, rather than as they *appear to be*, we know the Son of God, not as good or bad, sick or well, rich or poor, but as Spirit—living and moving and having his being in God consciousness, dwelling in the secret place of the most High. This is loving God supremely, this is loving our neighbor as ourself, and this is the fulfilling of the law of love. If we love God, and if we love the Son of God, we will serve our fellow-man, awakening him to the understanding of his true identity. Although we may temporarily and humanly assist him, while so doing we will know, through the inner discernment which is faith, that the kingdom of God within him is breaking through to his conscious awareness so that he, too, may know "the love of Christ which passeth all knowledge," and that he, too, "might be filled with all the fulness of God."

Whether we ever walk this earth in the spiritual light of realized demonstration, or whether, at some periods, we walk through the dark valley, always we must know this truth: "I will never leave thee, nor forsake thee"—the divine Presence goeth before me to make the crooked places straight. I have meat the world knoweth not: therefore, I will not fear mortal man; I will not fear circumstances or conditions. Christ, at the center of my individual being, is my strength. Faith is our ability to feel the nearness of the presence of God, and to walk confidently with Him. Faith is our realization of Emmanuel, God with us, as all good. Through faith we have the spiritual meat and bread of life, even though physical sense may sometimes testify to its absence. In moments of illumination and uplifted consciousness, it is easy to voice the Christ; but faith is demonstrated when, in the temporary barrenness and emptiness, we are able to discern the divine Light within. When the world cries out in despair, "I am fearful; I am in sin; I am in poverty," the wise one, the one whose faith is pure and holy, looks through these appearances and sees only the presence of the Christ.

*   *   *

"And the angel answered and said unto her, The Holy Ghost shall come upon thee, and the power of the Highest shall overshadow thee: therefore also that holy thing which shall be born of thee shall be called the Son of God." This is not an historical event of two thousand years ago: this is an eternal revelation from on High, and it is being addressed to you and to me, today. "The Holy Ghost shall come upon thee, and the power of the Highest shall overshadow thee." When we experience the divine visitation of the Christ, we are aware that we can do all things through the Spirit of God that is within us. In this moment of realizing the Presence, with its release from care and discord, with the healing of sin and disease, the Holy Ghost has come upon us, and the power of the Highest has overshadowed us, and it is then that we have experienced the birth of the Christ in human awareness. If our reliance is wholly and entirely upon the Spirit, we realize that release and healing as an activity of the Christ, an overshadowing of the power of God, a descent of the Holy Ghost. Then we know that the Christ has been received in consciousness, and that It has done Its work. There is no spiritual healing until the moment of the descent of the Holy Ghost, and it is in that moment that the error is dispelled, and the dream of illusion is broken.

In all humility, we wait for the descent of the Holy Ghost, the overshadowing of His presence, that by the riches of His glory we may be strengthened with might by His Spirit in the inner man— "that Christ may dwell in your hearts by faith; that ye, being rooted and grounded in love, may be able to comprehend with all saints what is the breadth, and length, and depth, and height: and to know the love of Christ, which passeth all knowledge, that ye might be filled with all the fulness of God."

The Monastic Life

Cut off from all emotional attachments, knowing no deep devotion to any person or thing, one may live the monastic life while still *in* the world, but not *of* it.

Often the monastic life is lived with a deep concern for mankind—with the desire to uplift, serve, and sometimes save the world—yet there is no deep love for any individual, nor is there a *need* for mother, brother, wife, or friend.

Many who "give up the world" to abide in a monastery or convent find that complete separation from loved ones, or from being loved, is beyond their power. There has not yet come to them the necessary insulation from worldly love and care. The monastic life, even when lived in the world, is completely insulated so that there is no emotional interchange in human relationships. In this spiritual insulation, one lives in devotion to human service and spiritual regeneration—but without involvement in personal emotions. It is this spiritual insulation which makes possible the life of aloneness lived by mystics. Yet, the very qualities emanating from the mystic's aloneness are the blessing to all who touch, or are touched by, the mystic's life. Emotion would be a drain, depleting the spiritual power inherent in the true monastic life.

It is doubtful if the monastic life can be cultivated. It is a gift of God, bestowed upon those ready for the experience, and always it is for a specific purpose. One possessing it may have remaining hidden longings for closer companionship with those of his family or religious circles, and sometimes even a deep desire for home—but he has not the capacity to enjoy or remain in them. Often these human desires are leaks in the insulation, or a leftover from the last human experience on earth.

It is this inability to fuse that makes the mystic

difficult to live or work with. Always the spiritual light serves as a barrier to emotional reaction—and for the sake of his friends and relatives, it would be better for one living the monastic life to separate himself from personal contacts. Then the impersonal life of Love is lived without strain or drain upon one's sources of spiritual power.

Only the emotions strain or drain the spiritual capacities, and these are absent when the monastic life is lived apart from family experience. Since all those called to the monastic life are not drawn to the monastery or convent, it is wise to thus withdraw from too close contact with ordinary human living.

Many who are drawn to the monastic life retain for many years the longing for one—one companion, friend, parent, wife, or husband—just someone with whom to share every unfolding inner experience and outer fruitage. A "dark night of the Soul," which may last many weeks, brings the final release from all attachments, and the monastic life is lived fully in God. Now all human associations and relationships are as impersonal, yet as warm and tender, as that of God to man.

The Bridge Over Which We Travel

We are living in a new religious age—new, not in the sense of modern, but new in the sense of renewal, re-establishment, revival, restatement. From Lao-tse, Krishna and Buddha; from Jesus, John, and Paul; from St. Augustine, St. Teresa, and Brother Lawrence; from Boehme, Eckhart, and Fox, up to the present day, always the message of salvation has been the same—*The kingdom of God is within you!* The Infinite Way is a restatement of the eternal truth that within you is the hidden manna, the meat that does not perish, the springs of eternal life; that within you there is an invisible Source of life, protection, supply, peace, harmony, and love. In other words, all the capacities for your spiritual growth and for your material well-being are already established within your own individual being. The Infinite Way presents a faith in, and an understanding of, an invisible principle that knows no religious bounds. God is one God—universal, impersonal, impartial, ever available, omnipotent, before Abraham, here and now, and unto eternity. Anyone on the face of the earth may have recourse to this infinite Source of all good. It matters not whether one is a Hebrew or a Christian, a Mohammedan or a Buddhist, a saint or a sinner—it is only necessary that one learn the truth of this great and unfailing principle and rely upon it. Everyone who turns to the spiritual kingdom, opening his consciousness to the activity and power of the Christ within, can touch and tap this source of Life; and as these spiritual faculties are opened, and impartation of the Spirit received and accepted, spiritual enrichment and enlightenment, healing and supply take place.

Many people who have been truth students for years querulously and wistfully ask: "Why do I still have so many problems?" In answer, I can truthfully say that it is because their study has been entirely in the realm of the mind—therefore, the heart has not been opened, and the great reservoir of the Soul remains untouched. Paul, in his great wisdom, said: "But now we are delivered from the law, that being dead wherein we were held; that we should serve in newness of spirit, and not in the oldness of the letter. . . . Not that we are sufficient of ourselves to think any thing as of ourselves; but our sufficiency is of God; Who also hath made us able ministers of the new testament; not of the letter, but of the spirit: for the letter killeth, but the spirit giveth life." It is true, of course, that students who sincerely study spiritual literature develop a certain degree of awareness or Christ consciousness, and those who are willing to devote more time and endeavor to the practice and application of what they study will go further and deeper into consciousness. Everything you learn from the written and spoken word strengthens and increases the degree of your spiritual awareness, and each is a step leading up to the ultimate goal—the realization of God. However, if you rely solely upon what you read or can declare and recite from memory, your reliance is placed entirely upon the letter of truth, and the letter is not the healing agency. However, if you use the letter of truth as a means to open your consciousness to the inflow of the divine Word of God, it will only be a short time until the spiritual flow will come forth from the infinite Source within your own being.

Three times the Master fed the multitudes, but still the people failed to perceive the spiritual principle behind the miracles. "Why reason ye, because ye have no bread? perceive ye not yet, neither understand? have ye your heart yet hardened?

Having eyes, see ye not? and having ears, hear ye not? and do ye not remember? . . . Verily, verily, I say unto you, Ye seek me, not because ye saw the miracle, but because ye did eat of the loaves, and were filled. Labour not for the meat which perisheth, but for that meat which endureth unto everlasting life, which the Son of man shall give unto you: for him hath God the Father sealed.''

Repeated failures and disappointments have taught us that nothing attained or accomplished in the outer world constitutes satisfaction or completeness, for even after achieving our worldly aims and ambitions there still remained a deep hunger and a great thirst—inwardly there was a void, an emptiness. And so it is that those of us who have resolutely set our feet upon the spiritual path press ever onward and upward, because we have found a degree of the peace that passeth understanding and a measure of the meat that leaves us not an hungered. We have found that our security, safety, peace, and satisfaction are not to be found in persons, places, circumstances, or things. Our good is found and realized in that which the world would call an intangible—the Spirit of God within us, the Christ of our own being, whereby we contact that which appears outwardly as the health of our bodies, the dollars in our purse, the homes wherein we dwell, the companions in whom we joy. Therefore, our dependence is not upon the visible universe.

As we witness the abundance of all nature, we realize that our reliance is not upon these *things*, but upon the invisible *Principle* that produced them. We look not to our present supply, occupation, or resources, but always to the invisible Source from whence they came. As we look only to the invisible Presence and Power that produced manna in the wilderness, oil in the widow's cruse, the five loaves and the few fishes, we find that our good, whether it be supply, home, harmony, or health, is forthcoming. We are fruitful, successful, and joyous in proportion as our reliance is ever on the Infinite Invisible. "For faith is the substance of things hoped for, the evidence of things not seen."

The Master revealed: "Before Abraham was, I am." This Spirit is universal truth, and it was this Spirit that produced manna and water for Moses; that appeared as food for Elijah, that raised Jesus Christ from the dead, and it is this same Spirit that will quicken also your mortal body. All this is an activity of the Spirit of God, the Christ, which has existed before the world began, and which will continue unto the end of the world, before Abraham and unto the end of the world—a continuous state of *is-ness*—which makes this Spirit a matter of the present, the *now!*

"And he said, So is the kingdom of God, as if a man should cast seed into the ground; And should sleep, and rise night and day, and the seed should spring and grow up, he knoweth not how. For the earth bringeth forth fruit of herself; first the blade, then the ear, after that the full corn in the ear. But when the fruit is brought forth, immediately he putteth in the sickle, because the harvest is come. And he said, Whereunto shall we liken the kingdom of God? or with what comparison shall we compare it? It is like a grain of mustard seed, which, when it is sown in the earth, is less than all the seeds that be in the earth: But when it is sown, it groweth up, and becometh greater than all herbs, and shooteth out great branches; so that the fowls of the air may lodge under the shadow of it." Mark 4:26-32.

As you diligently search for the kingdom of God, it is right and fitting that those who have found and entered therein should give unto you healing, supply, and harmony—the waters of life—until you have had the opportunity to receive and understand the principle for yourself. Thus it is that the material that has been presented in these monthly letters can be used to great advantage, because each *Letter* is a lesson in expanding the understanding that *the kingdom of God is within you.* In everyday language they present an opportunity to drink from the fount of living waters, thereby opening consciousness to receive the revelation of truth from within your own being. Each has but one object: the deepening and ripening of your individual consciousness, that the spiritual activity of the Christ may be awakened in you, so that you may go out into the world and be the light of life and love unto all men. These letters form a bridge over which you travel in your journey from sense to Soul, and after you have crossed this bridge you will find yourself in the Promised Land—within your own being you will find yourself at-one with God—". . . the place whereon thou standest is holy ground. . . . Son, thou art ever with me, and all that I have is thine." Again and again this principle of oneness with God has been presented and reiterated, in numerous ways and by means of various illustrations, always endeavoring to make you realize that the kingdom you seek is not to be found anywhere external to your own being.

Throughout the ages, men in search of God have made the pilgrimage to Mecca, to Jerusalem, to Rome, only to find that the Master's words are true: ". . . believe me, the hour cometh, when ye shall neither in this mountain, nor yet at Jerusalem, worship the Father . . . the true worshippers shall worship the Father in spirit and in truth: for the Father seeketh such to worship him. God is a Spirit: and they that worship him must worship him in spirit and in truth.

"Jesus cried and said, He that believeth on me, believeth not on me, but on him that sent me. And he that seeth me seeth him that sent me. I am come a light into the world, that whosoever believeth on me should not abide in darkness." John 12:44-6.

P.O. Box 5308.

Honolulu,
Hawaii.

PUBLISHER'S NOTE

The Infinite Way is now published by DeVorss & Company. *The Art of Meditation* and *Practicing the Presence* are now published by HarperCollins, San Francisco.

Joel Goldsmith wrote over forty books and essays over the many years of his teaching activities. All Goldsmith writings currently in print are available from DeVorss & Company.